I
ALONE
HAVE ESCAPED
TO TELL YOU

RALPH McINERNY

I
ALONE
HAVE ESCAPED
TO TELL YOU

MY LIFE AND PASTIMES

UNIVERSITY OF NOTRE DAME PRESS

NOTRE DAME, INDIANA

Copyright © 2006 by University of Notre Dame
Notre Dame, Indiana 46556
www.undpress.nd.edu
All Rights Reserved

Manufactured in the United States of America

Library of Congress Cataloging in-Publication Data

McInerny, Ralph M.
I alone have escaped to tell you : my life and pastimes / Ralph McInerny.
p.   cm.
ISBN-13: 978-0-268-03492-4 (alk. paper)
ISBN-10: 0-268-03492-3 (alk. paper)
1. McInerny, Ralph M.   2. McInerny, Ralph M.—Friends and associates.
3. Novelists, American—20th century—Biography.   4. Catholic authors—
United States—Biography.   5. College teachers—United States—Biography.
6. University of Notre Dame—Biography.   I. Title.
PS3563.A31166Z46   2006
813'.54—dc22

2006000840

∞ *This book is printed on acid-free paper.*

In Memoriam

uxoris meae Constantiae

Autobiographies are not really serious in the way novels are.

—Kingsley Amis

The best of a bad job is all the most of us make of it—except of course the saints.

—T. S. Eliot

Forsan et haec olim meminisse juvabit.

—Virgil

CONTENTS

REFLECTIONS
IN A GOLDEN I

TO SAY THAT THIS BOOK IS NOT THE *CONFESSIONS* OF ST. AUGUSTINE may sound as gratuitous as saying that none of my novels is *War and Peace,* but the remark has point. In writing these memoirs I have been conscious of the fact that I am not writing the story of a soul; that would be an altogether more depressing exercise. The septuagenarian finds self-delusion difficult, and there is an account of my life that could be of interest only to God and myself. Remember Augustine's addressee. Only a saint could be so unflinchingly honest about his life, and I—another needless disclaimer—am no saint. What I have written is the truth, but of course it is not the whole truth, not even the fuller grasp I myself might have of it. Even for that, I would want to invoke St. Paul's *neque meipsum iudico,* his admission that he remained largely a mystery to himself and was even unable to say for certain that he was in the state of grace.

When friends of mine suggested that I write an autobiography I was at first amused. But the thought grew on me, as unfriendly suggestions will, and I imagined writing little bursts on the order of the End Notes I did for each issue of *Crisis*: episodes, people, events, arranged more or less chronologically, but not aiming at any narrative control beyond before and after. The thought enabled me to begin. What emerged is not quite that, but it is close. I recall the past in terms of large categories that enable me to gather together events and activities and people. Of course there is some transgression of genera. The account has a beginning, a middle, and, if not an end, brings matters to where the shadows have lengthened, the sun sinks slowly in the west, and I find myself praying for mercy and the grace of a happy death.

Autobiography is very likely the most various of literary genres. It includes the confessional account—edifying like St. Augustine's, the opposite in the case of Rousseau's, corrupt as practiced by Anaïs Nin and Henry Miller, incredible in the case of Frank Harris. Chesterton's seems to be about everyone but himself, as in a way is that of Kingsley Amis. Most of Amis's chapters bear the names of the persons and places he chooses to pillory and excoriate. The targets of these witty put-downs could scarcely enjoy them, but the reader is soon in the grips of morose delectation. Outright laughter, actually. But then Amis is pretty hard on himself as well.

Collections of letters are more unbuttoned, even more so diaries, particularly when they were kept without any thought of eventual publication. I would mention Evelyn Waugh's letters to Nancy Mitford and Diana Cooper, but he seems to have assumed these more or less pagan ladies were preserving his letters. Why this difference? The autobiography, excepting Augustine's, perhaps, is a device that enables the writer to give a carefully edited version of his passage through time. But even Augustine fails to mention the name of Adeodatus's mother. Graham Greene apparently forgot the names of his children. The autobiographer's besetting temptation is summed up in Nietzsche's question, "Why am I so wonderful?" If life is a book in which one sets out to write one story and ends by writing another, an autobiography tends to be an account which, if not hagiographical, seldom puts the writer in the dock. Even recounting unflattering episodes can seem a preemptive strike.

I began this task reluctantly but soon was taking culpable pleasure in the exercise. Aristotle distinguished between memory and reminiscence, and I began to see what he meant. A hitherto forgotten past—people, places, events—suddenly comes vividly to mind, emerging from who knows what recesses of the self. The greatest problem is to find a principle of exclusion. So much of what comes flooding back can scarcely interest anyone but myself. It is the thought that much of the contents of memory will be interred with one's bones that spurs one on. If nothing else, this record may be of interest to my children and grandchildren.

Because the real story of one's life is known only to God, few autobiographers put themselves in His presence as they write. The shaping of events makes one acutely aware of the mystery of even the most ordinary human life. "Know thyself" is not only the slogan for the most difficult task of all; it is one few of us care to undertake. The autobiographer becomes increasingly aware that he is plucking items from a vast underground river, the course of which he only dimly perceives. He comes to see that his can only be a partial account, not simply because the whole is quantitatively unmanageable, but because the sense of the whole is hidden from him.

I find that the effort to write one's own life induces a deep skepticism about biographies. As 2003 turned into 2004, sunning myself on Longboat Key, I read a lot of biographies as distraction from, perhaps as a spur to, writing these memoirs. There are wonderful bookstores in Sarasota, and I would periodically bring back a bushel basket of remaindered and discounted volumes to my sybaritic condo. Over the space of a few weeks, I read the lives of Oscar Wilde, of John Gray, of Emily Dickinson, of Wilkie Collins, of Jonathan Swift and Laurence Sterne. All of them were efforts to reconstruct a person from data available in archives and private collections, from the letters and the reminiscences of others. Research projects, in short. Someone emerges from such narratives, but the reader is usually more conscious of the writer than of the subject. Sterne was in his way the Andrew Greeley of his day (although to state the obverse would be libelous), but what one gets is a version of something essentially unknown. That we cannot get at the full truth of our own lives makes biography seem a branch of fiction. Attempts at a final judgment seem wildly presumptuous and finally impossible.

For all that, I love biography, particularly literary biography. And I have become perhaps too fond of writing my memoirs. Jude Dougherty and I once entered into a pact to write one another's obituaries—lest the truth come out. It turns out that there is little danger of that. It is not simply that friends have an honorable tendency to see the best in one another. In reflective moments, when one gets an intimation of what one looks like to God, it is a relief to have the moment pass. Such narratives as this are all, in a way, what Newman called the history of his religious opinions, an apologia pro vita sua. One is making a case in the hope that it is, if far from the whole truth, nonetheless true.

BIOSPHERE

WHERE I GREW UP, THE MISSISSIPPI RIVER DIVIDES MINNEAPOLIS from St. Paul; lower down in Lake City, where my great-great-grandfather Patrick and his wife Nora are buried, the river separates Minnesota from Wisconsin; on a map, it cuts the whole country in two. The Mississippi takes its rise from Lake Itasca in northern Minnesota, an unpromising beginning, and then broadens and winds its way to New Orleans and the Gulf of Mexico. In imagination and memory, it just keeps rolling along.

Patrick and Nora left Ennis in County Clare, Ireland, in either 1844 or 1845 and settled for some twenty years near Perth, Ontario, before descending to Lake City, where they are located by the U.S. Census of 1870. My great-grandfather Austin Joseph also lived in Lake City following his marriage to Mary Connell in Louisville, but the family moved on to Minneapolis after a spell of farming near De Graff, Minnesota, one of the communities founded by Archbishop John Ireland of St. Paul in order to get the Irish out of the wicked cities and back to the land where they belong. (I owe this genealogical lore to my brother Steve.)

Maurice Patrick, my grandfather on my father's side, was successful in both business and politics in Minneapolis. My mother said of him that he was the nicest man she ever knew. He died the year I was born. My father, another Austin—certain names recur in the family with the occasional antic departure like my own—married Vivian Rush in 1926. Nine of their children survived, and indeed all are still living as I write.

During World War II, my father built tankers in Chaska with Cargill Corporation and once traveled on a completed vessel down the river to New Orleans. When I enlisted in the Marine Corps in 1946, it was a tossup whether one was sent to San Diego or Parris Island for boot camp. My brother Ray had been sent to North Carolina. I was sent to San Diego. The Twin Cities are both east and west of the river, and the Marine Corps vacillated on considering recruits from there western or eastern. Wherever I have gone, wherever I have lived, the Mississippi has dominated the country of my mind.

Whenever I reread *Huckleberry Finn,* which is almost every year, it is like going home, although Huck's is the only raft I have ever been on. The evocation of the antebellum river is only part of the attraction. *Life on the Mississippi* is far more evocative of those times. Mark Twain lived most of his life away from his town of origin, and when he did return to Hannibal, Missouri, late in life, he seemed ill at ease in a present that obscured the past. When I saw that little town on the western bank of the Mississippi for the first time, on my way to a stint as visiting professor at Truman State in Missouri, I could understand why Mark Twain went back there only once, with ambiguous results. Maybe it was more than merely the passage of time, but the river inhabits the innocence of childhood and can seem to mock tragic old age. Twain had lost his wife and daughter and seemed unable to stave off the despair that not even suits of ice-cream white could diminish.

When I was a boy, the Mississippi at first seemed a tributary of Minnehaha Creek, which starts in Lake Minnetonka and runs through Minneapolis to the famous falls and on to the river. Lake of the Isles, Lake Calhoun, Lake Harriet, Lake Nokomis, Lake Hiawatha, and others are linked by the creek, making a vast park of half of Minneapolis. My grandfather had been an alderman when the great system of parks was formed and Minnehaha Creek conceded eminent domain. Just below our street, the creek flowed through what seemed like a vast meadow, though we lived in the heart of the city. There were tennis courts, and in the evening my father practiced iron shots along the creek. My brother Maurice fell off the footbridge when he was only a toddler and floated hundreds of yards, as blissful as Ophelia, before he was fished out. "There is a willow grows aslant a brook. . . . " I already had an image for those words when I first read them, as if Hamlet's beloved had drifted down Minnehaha Creek. A replica of Longfellow's house, a branch of the public library, overlooked a skating rink just above the falls.

It has been said that you cannot step twice into the same river; that goes for creeks as well. But that is only literally true. Like the snows of yesteryear, such waterways are gone forever yet ever present. "A boy's will is the wind's will, and the thoughts of youth are long long thoughts." Those of age are even longer.

■   I came into the world in February 1929, a half year before the Great Depression. I do not suggest a causal connection. I was born at home, on 36th Avenue in South Minneapolis, delivered by my uncle Maurice. I was the third child in what would eventually be a family of nine children. (A sister, also delivered at home by my Uncle Maurice, died almost immediately, but I am sure my parents always thought they had ten children.) So in my own family, after we lost our firstborn, Michael, my six surviving children were taught to think, in the words of Wordsworth's poem, we are seven.

My grandfather Maurice Patrick, a pillar of the parish of St. Helena, alderman of the ward, and successful businessman—M. P. McInerny Heating and Plumbing was located at 513 Fourth Avenue South in downtown Minneapolis—died in 1929, and that fact, coupled with the Depression, plunged us into something very close to poverty. But that was a common fate. Whether this is due to poor memory or a lack of imagination, the realization surprises me. I look back on my childhood as a veritable idyll of happiness.

I went off to kindergarten, at John Ericson School, from 2810 E. Minnehaha Parkway, a house my grandfather had built. After his death, my father and my uncle Clate tried to run his business, but by stages they lost everything, and my most vivid memories are of 4034 27th Avenue, where we lived from my first into my eighth year in the parish school.

As I have said, winding through my early years is Minnehaha Creek. Even when we lived on 27th Avenue, we were but a block's walk from it where it feeds first into and then out of Lake Hiawatha. (In my father's childhood it was called Rice Lake.) It feeds my memories now of the years before I went off to Nazareth Hall in 1942, at the age of thirteen—and of many later memories as well. After my discharge from the Marine Corps, I spent the summer of 1947 lolling on the main beach of Lake Nokomis, courtesy of the veterans' program called 52/20, so called because if one succeeded in remaining unemployed, the government supplied twenty dollars a week for a year. It was not a negligible sum in those days, at least for one content to sport with Amaryllis in the sun.

My original sin had the creek for its setting. As I walked home from school along the muddy banks in spring, one of my rubbers became stuck, and I stepped out of it and continued home. On the way, I discarded the other rubber. Where were my rubbers? I said they had been stolen. But the great sin was to accuse a kid named Tony of having taken them. As it happened, Tony's family were not held in high repute, and my story was believed, if not by my mother, by my visiting Aunt Charlotte—one or the other of my mother's sisters spent greater or lesser lengths of time in our home—and my lie stirred her moral indignation. Over my mother's protests, she marched me off to Tony's home. During the walk I must have found her mood contagious, learning for the first time how an interested lie can have all the allure of the truth. Charlotte pounded on the door and a wary, harried woman answered. From behind Tony's mother came the not yet hushed sounds of her many children. My aunt declared our purpose. Tony was summoned by his mother and just stared at me when the accusation was made. Of course he denied it, but not even his mother believed him. She gave him a whack and he disappeared. My aunt demanded the rubbers. Somehow the incident ended, my aunt apparently satisfied that Tony's mother acknowledged her son was a thief, and we went home. My own mother seemed to sense that her son was a liar, and I confessed to her that night when she put me to bed. The memory of that lie and false accusation has never gone away. It is firmly embedded in the bottom stratum of my self, representing the day when I achieved what moralists call the Age of Reason and walked for the first time out of the garden of innocence.

We swam in the lakes and skated on them in winter, played hockey and baseball, and in season our team, The Bluebirds, entered in the schedule arranged by the park board at the pavilion at Lake Hiawatha. We fished, we retrieved golf balls hit over the fence of Hiawatha golf course, and we sold them back to the players. I hawked newspapers on a corner before school began, three cents a copy, earning a pittance, but later went on to a paper route, which was far more lucrative. That entailed collecting money from the customers on my route once a week. In those days, Minneapolis newspapers had metal shacks scattered through the city, at which the papers were doled out to the paperboys. We did not leave the shack until we had folded each paper and stuffed them in the cloth bags we carried as we flung them at our customers' doors. The small amounts my brothers and I earned played an important role in the domestic economy. The new clothes bought at the beginning of a school year were paid for with our earnings.

But what I most remember is the indolence of those days, particularly in summer. There were the sports I mentioned, and there were long hikes. And books. The Roosevelt branch of the Minneapolis Public Library was visible from our screened front porch on 27th Avenue, which was a favorite shaded place. During the summer the library organized reading programs, and one earned stars of different colors for the amount one read, which could be proudly presented to the nun when school resumed. Every three years or so, residential streets were ploughed and then resurfaced and oiled, filling the air with fragrance. Ice and milk and other foodstuffs were brought to the door, sometimes drawn by horses, who left mementos in the street. I particularly remember the horsedrawn Bamby Wagon, bringing bread and pastry, and the Jewel Tea man.

I have learned that my own children become skeptical when I describe the jobs of my own childhood—selling newspapers, delivering them, caddying at the Minnikada Club overlooking Lake Calhoun. What I could not convey, apparently, was how wonderful it was. The early morning hawking of newspapers is eclipsed by the memory of sitting on the screen porch reading the books I brought home from the library. Many years later, I took my father on a little tour of the stations of our life, and we stopped at the Roosevelt library. Some of my own things were on the computer, and my father's delight at this became my own. Any tendency on my part to doubt the idyllic memories of my grade school years is swept away whenever I revisit Minneapolis and drive along Minnehaha Parkway, which runs beside the creek from Lake Harriet to my old neighborhood. Thousands and thousands of middle-class homes look out on vistas that would be rare and costly elsewhere.

After half a year of kindergarten at John Ericson School, begun before my fifth birthday, I entered the parish school of St. Helena's Church, where I would spend the next eight years. We were taught by Sisters of St. Joseph of Carondolet. The parish had not yet built a convent, and the sisters lived in the school, in space across from the classrooms on the second floor. They had a little chapel and once a week, on Monday, Father Rowan the pastor would say his 6:45 a.m. Mass there; boys assigned as his servers for the week began the Mass in that little chapel. It has become fashionable to grouse about the nuns in parish schools, and there has been much nonsense and libel spread abroad. In the course of my eight years I had seven different nuns, and with with one possible exception—we called her Sister Sour Grapefruit—they were a cheerful community, which, given their living conditions, is amazing, and they were good teachers. Like us, they dreamt of summer, for then they could return to St. Catherine's College in St. Paul and a comparatively posh existence.

Students in the parish school assumed that they were miles ahead of the poor devils attending John Ericson across the street, a school we somehow thought of as the Protestant school. Sister Ellen Joseph taught me in both the seventh and eighth grades, moving up to teach the eighth when she became principal. Along the way to that final year I developed a taste for history and literature, thanks to Sister Rose Alma. Boxes of books were delivered to the school each week, often with copies of one of the Father Francis Finn stories—*Tom Playfair, Percy Wynn*—and we eagerly read them. We learned how to sing, we learned how to diagram sentences, we learned our catechism.

The only story I could tell on the nuns took place when I was in first grade and had not yet mastered the mystery of *R*. My teacher, Sister Mary Electa, would take me up the hall to other nuns and I would be put through a little ritual. What is your name? Walph. What are your brothers' names? Woger and Waymond. There was nothing cruel in this; they obviously found my lisping cute, and I would be hugged and taken back to my desk. A few years later I startled my mother by asking if the nuns were defeminized—I think I used this word. The question was prompted by the absence of bosom in the nun I had in second grade. I could rattle off the names of the nuns I had, but I won't. They are all now consigned to the Tomb of the Unknown Nun. But I remember them all. More importantly, God does.

My Uncle Maurice had one of the first home movie cameras, and my dad got one of his own as soon as he could afford it. It is because of this that I can watch myself and my brothers frisking for the camera at 2810 E. Minnehaha Parkway and later at 4034 27th Avenue. There is no theme to this footage, and the camera jolts and jumps from one scene to another with no continuity. This is part of its charm, since the very amateurishness contributes to the notion that one is eavesdropping on the past. Still photographs are wonderful, but movies have an eerie capacity to evoke the past. Old men are children once again, my father is theatrically handsome, my mother radiant and fruitful. Rog and Ray stage a boxing match, Babe (Austin junior) walks in and out of the picture, Denny bounces around, and I sit smiling amidst them, more of an observer than a participant. Mary Margaret was the baby then, Theresa and Maurice and Stephen not having yet arrived. My brother Ray has amalgamated all those old films and put them on videos. Nostalgia is only a moment away. I sit and control the past—stop, rewind, play again—my finger on the appropriately named remote control. Eventually the subject of these movies is family weddings, my own among them, so that I can watch Connie and me emerge from St. Thomas Church on January 3, 1953, again and again, and see her throw her flowers, which were caught by Eloise soon to be McDonald, the wife of my best man. My father-in-law could not wait to get out of his formal dress, and he appears in the pictures taken afterwards at the Kunert home in a woolen shirt. Raised a Lutheran, he had not been inside any church for years before he walked Connie down the aisle, so maybe that unusual experience also sped him home before the rest of us.

■   I was in first grade when I became one of the six so-called choirboys who, wearing cassock and surplice, sat on benches in the sanctuary during the Sunday High Mass. Just sat there. We did nothing else, certainly not sing. The next step was becoming an altar boy, and that meant memorizing the Latin responses. The prayers at the foot of the altar were the real test, the priest and altar boy rapidly exchanging verses of Psalm 42— *Introibo ad altare Dei, ad Deum qui laetificat iuventutem meam*—and then there was the bowed recitation of the Confiteor. Once the priest mounted to the altar it was comparatively easy. One had to be on the alert to move the book from the epistle to the gospel side, as we called them—the priest would signal by laying his hand on the linen surface. The altar missal was huge, and one carried it on its stand, descending to the foot of the altar, genuflecting, then mounting to place it on the opposite side. One then stood until the priest began to read, then bowed and returned to the foot of the altar. From time to time, a boy would step on his cassock as he was carrying the book and tumble on the stairs.

The daily Masses were at 6:45, 7:30 and 8:00 a.m., the first said by Father Rowan, the others by his assistants. In 1940, freshly ordained, Paul J. Gorman was assigned to St. Helena's. One of his tasks was to take charge of the altar boys, and we formed the St. John Berchman's Society. I was made president, to my genuine surprise. Gorman had what in those days was thought of as a late vocation, being twenty-eight when he was ordained. He came from Maple Lake, Minnesota, and was a gifted musician who had been the organist during his seminary days. When the new St. Helena's Church was built with a magnificent organ, Father Gorman would sometimes go up in the loft and play his heart out to an empty church. The sound would reach us across the intervening playground: Dr. Vibes. He was a strange fellow, and I became one of his favorites. He did not own a car, so when he took some of us to the Nankin Restaurant downtown for a massive meal of Chinese food costing a total of $1.25 each, we went by street car or, *mirabile dictu,* by cab. It was under the influence of Father Gorman and Sister Ellen Joseph that I began to think of the priesthood. Father Gorman gave me a Short Breviary, a beautiful volume published by the Benedictines at St. John's in Collegeville, Minnesota, an order Gorman had once thought of joining. I still have the book. In eighth grade, on Sundays in spring, I would carry it as I crossed the Ford Bridge and walked up the river road on the St. Paul side to Summit Avenue to attend vespers in the seminary chapel. The sight of the seminarians processing across the grounds in their cassocks and surplices, birettas set at various angles on their heads, in their hands a *Liber Usualis,* stirred me. It was like a recruiting poster in living tableau. And so it was decided that I might enter Nazareth Hall, the minor seminary of the archdiocese of St. Paul, after I graduated from eighth grade.

THREE

SPOILED PRIEST

NAZARETH HALL STOOD ON THE SHORE OF LAKE JOHANNA, NORTH OF
St. Paul, out Snelling Avenue from the fairgrounds. That was where the
street car line stopped in the fall of 1947 when I set off for my old school
on foot, thereby impressing the rector Father Shanahan and doubtless
making him more amenable to my request that I be readmitted to Nazareth Hall. I had already spent the best years of my youth here.

The seminary system of the archdiocese of St. Paul in those days
comprised twelve years, six of them to be spent at the preparatory seminary, Nazareth Hall, and the rest at the major seminary on Summit Avenue and the River Road in St. Paul. As I noted earlier, in the spring of my
eighth grade I sometimes walked from home to the chapel of the seminary on Sundays to watch the seminarians process into chapel for vespers, clad in their cassocks and surplices and birettas. Sister Ellen Joseph
made sure that the boys in her class knew of the possibility of a vocation.
Looking through the bulletins from various seminaries, I was struck by
their *horaria*. Each day was ordered by the hour, from rising to going to
bed. Four boys from my eighth-grade class went off to Nazareth Hall: Eu-
gene Schmidt, John Johnson, Art Hesburg, and myself. In the event, none
of us was ordained (although our classmate Marvin Deutsch became a

Maryknoll missionary), but then, the point of the prolonged system was to give one an opportunity to make a careful decision. I had left Nazareth Hall after three years and joined the Marine Corps (of which more later), and now I wanted to return. I had lolled on the main beach at Lake Nokomis, I had put in a quarter term at the University of Minnesota, but I was dissatisfied.

When I entered Nazareth Hall in 1942 I was thirteen years old, a First Year boy. Each year received its ordinal designation, suggesting a continuum that ran through high school into the first two years of college. My heroes were upperclassmen, especially those college men who held positions of prominence—head prefect, head waiter, editor of the *Puer Nazarenus,* even the student barber, Don Schnitizius—and I became a kind of pet during my first year. For one thing I was small, naïve, and sassy. One of my assignments, fulfilled on Sunday morning between the low Mass and the high Mass, was to take a pitcher of holy water along the college corridor and fill the little fonts inside each door. After knocking, I would open the door and call out, *Ecce aqua benedicta.* To which the reply was *Sit nobis salus et vita.* As the year went on, I intoned my message to the opening notes of "My Darling Clementine" until, when the novelty wore off, a disapproving frown or two told me that laughter could be had at too high a price.

One of the agonizing aspects of my first year at Nazareth Hall was the fact that I did not have a suit. It was specified in the list of clothing to bring along, but my mother apparently thought it was optional—a thirteen-year-old wearing a suit? I had two sweaters, one red and one green, which I alternated. It was only on Sunday that the lack of a suit mattered, since that is the day one dressed up, but I was dressed as I always was. However keenly I felt this—and in my own mind the humiliation was magnified—I never said a word to my mother. How proud she had been when they brought me to school and she came up to the First-Year dorm to get me settled.

Because of our small size, Johnnie Johnson and I were chosen by Father Casey to serve benediction in the sisters' chapel in the afternoon. The service could not have occurred every day, but I forget which days it was. In any case, we would set off from Father Casey's freshman English class and march through the refectory into the kitchen, where double doors admitted us to the convent wing. The place was spick and span, but the sacristy and sanctuary were Lilliputian in size, which was why the altar boys had to be small. When we arrived the nuns would already be at prayer in their heavy German accents. This was war time, and one of them, Sister Theotima, had a brother in the German navy, but Catholicism is catholic. How plaintive were their voices lifting in the Eucharistic hymns, their faces veiled. The little chapel was soon full of incense, and when Father Casey took the monstrance and turned to bless the nuns, I rang a bell vigorously.

Father Casey, a gifted, ascetic man—he was called a Detacher, after a movement started by a Pittsburgh priest, Father Hugo, who had a great influence on Dorothy Day—was also prefect of the First-Year dorm; each year one moved on to another dorm, until in Fifth Year one got a private room. The curriculum was classical—Latin from the very beginning, Greek starting in Third Year, English, history, math, science of a sort, and French or German. There were sports, of course, but I now accepted the fact that I would never shine in them. Besides, those on whom I began more or less consciously to model myself, even if they played basketball or hockey, were not known for that. They were writers. They published poems and stories in the *Puer Nazarenus*. I wonder if the issues of that magazine could still be found in some archives. Then I might learn how the poems of Leo Noterman would strike me now. At the time, they seemed the very standard of achievement. Leo was in the Fifth Year, and almost every month something by him appeared in the *Puer*. If I had had any notion of what a poet should look like, this good-looking but ordinary young man would have been puzzling.

This is when I first began to regard myself as a writer—in remote potency, as I would learn to say later. At the back of the study hall was a table and a few shelves containing reference books to save a trip to the library. Among them was Kunitz and Haycraft, *Twentieth-Century Authors*. It fascinated me. There were photographs the size of postage stamps of the authors with a double-column account of their lives, ending with a list of their books. I began to subtract the birthday of an author from the year of his first book. It was clear that most of them had begun publishing in their twenties, sometimes their early twenties. That gave me time.

We had nicknames for the faculty—Butch, Kush, Suki, Zip, Uncle Bill, Harpo, the Greek. They were all priests of the archdiocese who had been assigned to teach, a task most would do for perhaps fifteen years and then be rewarded with a parish. Almost none of them had advanced degrees, and in those days Nazareth Hall was not accredited, but they had been chosen because of their academic performance as seminarians. Some had the learning of autodidacts, a few were pursuing higher degrees, but by and large they spent the capital they had acquired as students and to which they had added since. This surprises me when I think of it now. Among them were some of the best teachers I ever had. Classics were at the heart of the curriculum. In Latin, after a year of grammar, we read Caesar, went on to Cicero, and then to Virgil and Horace. I was tutored in Catullus by Father Walter Peters, a vain and eccentric man shaped like the letter S, a German among so many Irish. He also taught me Horace and inspired me to read Thomas Mann. In Greek there was a year of grammar taught by Father Leo White (the Greek), who was also prefect of the study hall and spent afternoon and evening hours there, seated at a desk on a high platform, the better to survey his charges, a floor lamp beside his chair. He always seemed to be reading his breviary, either seated in the chair or pacing the outer aisles of the huge room, which held the entire high school. White was also director of the library, and I volunteered to work there, learning how to bind books and letter their spines according to the Dewey decimal system. The great attraction of the job was the books bequeathed by deceased priests; these arrived in huge boxes at regular intervals. Selections from these cornucopias added to my growing personal library. These were sanctioned acquisitions, by and large. But once I appropriated a beautiful *Imitatio Christi* bound in green leather with gilt-edged pages and a ribbon marker. I spirited it away without asking if I could. My conscience, aided by the irony of stealing a book on how to imitate Christ, led me to return it to the box from which I had taken it. I was so remorseful that I did not ask if I could take it legitimately. Every such donation would include a set of breviaries, often two sets, since a new Latin translation had been authorized by Pius XII, necessitating the purchase of four new volumes—one for each season—of the Roman Breviary. One of the principal tasks of a priest is to say his office, that is, read the hours of the day with their psalms and hymns and prayers and selections from the Fathers. In those days, this took more or less an hour. It seemed to take Father White several hours, but then, he was regularly interrupted by requests to go to the lavatory or to the library. During evening study hall, from 7:30 to 9 p.m., he was more sympathetic with the second request than the first.

The library was a long low room with a beamed ceiling that seemed aimed at the fireplace at the far end. In the center were huge library tables with lamps on them, and along the sides of the room were alcoves, each containing a little desk and chair and a window. Commandeering an alcove was the first order of business, then settling in. My reading during those years was affected by the books on the shelves of the alcove I happened to get. Stevenson's *Pueris Virginibusque* caught my eye, and I was a bit disappointed to find that the title meant simply For Boys and Girls. So that would have been in Second Year, when puberty had struck and heated thoughts occurred. After I read Proust, in English translation, I suggested to Father White that the volumes of Proust were inappropriate for our shelves, and he removed them. Well, keepers of the *Index librorum Prohibitorum* must first have read the books they forbade others to read.

But back to Greek. We went on from grammar to Xenophon and then to Homer's *Iliad*, after which we read St. Basil. Latin and Greek were deemed necessary for future priests, but there was no overt relating of our accumulating knowledge to our presumed future as priests. Doubtless it was assumed that the Latin liturgy was becoming intelligible to us as a result of our classical studies. Tubby Blatz, a disarmingly learned giant of a man, taught Plato to a small group of volunteers meeting in his room, where a Blatz Beer sign adorned one of the walls. He may have been the most naturally talented priest to teach at Nazareth Hall during my time there, but I never had the sense that he enjoyed his assignment. I still have Latin and Greek texts from that time. Scotchtaped to my Xenophon is an advertisement of a colorful bottle of Blatz beer. My Horace and Virgil from those days are on my shelves still, along with my Bennet's grammar and Cassell's Latin dictionary. My Xenophon also contains a marginal record of the "calls." When a student's name was called, he stood, read ten or fifteen lines, and then translated them, after which he was asked to parse a few words. Then on to the next call. The hope was that by keeping a record of the calls, it would be possible to predict when one's next turn would come. I don't think this ever proved true. I wrote a much appreciated doggerel poem which included the recurring line, "And Senta sits in front," which old friends from those days still remember. Senta was Bob Senta, who was eventually ordained for the Duluth diocese. A prudent man, he kept away from the back seats where rowdies gathered.

It is in the nature of such schools, perhaps all schools, that much of one's learning takes place independently of classes and teachers. For me, the *Puer Nazarenus* loomed large. We put on plays, of course, and once a year the faculty was seated in the front rows of the auditorium and subjected to ridicule. There were always mimics of uncanny ability who would bring down the house with imitations of one priest after another. Victims of such imitation never seemed to recognize what for everyone else were their distinctive traits. But it was the informal influence of such precocious and gifted students as Jerome Quinn and George Welzbacher, both a few years ahead of me, whose conversations opened up new possibilities, authors, projects. And Bob Klein and Marvin O'Connell and I began a novel; each of us would write a chapter and pass it on to one of the others for him to do the same, and so on. We hadn't written many chapters when we stopped. The plot was getting decidedly raunchy. Klein had been much taken by the cover photo of Truman Capote on *Other Voices, Other Rooms*—by the insolent languor, not the decadence.

In short, we were taught, but we also educated one another and ourselves. I was never caught up in the athletic side of the school, as most others were, and as far as I know neither Welzbacher nor Quinn ever raised a sweat from games or exercise. The late afternoon and evening walks out to the entry on Snelling Avenue and back consumed half an hour at least, and with four or five students together, conversation never lagged. When Thomas Merton's *Seven Storey Mountain* appeared in 1948, I was a college man. Its account of Merton's efforts to write novels struck me even more than the story of his conversion. After all, I had made a retreat at New Mount Mellary in Iowa with Father Gorman, so I probably thought I already knew something of Trappist monasteries. But Merton's account of the intellectual excitement of Columbia University was inspiring. (In the Marine Corps I had also read in a paperback service edition Mark Van Doren's *Liberal Education*. He was a great influence on Merton.) Most fascinating of all for me was Merton's withdrawal to the woods of upper New York, to a summer cottage with a few friends, each of whom was writing a novel.

We students were assigned various duties, such as serving Mass in the crypt where the faculty said their swift but licit private Masses at altars along both walls. (One could also go to confession any morning in the crypt, although confessors from outside were brought in on a weekly basis. Presumably a morning trip to the crypt spelled an emergency.) There were also outside work details, but the recurrent task was to wait tables in the refectory.

In those days everybody smoked, of course, but the rule of the school was that only the upper three years were permitted to do so. For underclassmen to be discovered smoking was in principle a cause for dismissal. A lean-to behind the study hall where tools and things were kept came to be called the Smoke Shack, for here the elect repaired at mid-morning for their between-classes cigarette and during the afternoon recreation period from three to four-thirty. The signs of rank and prestige are usually trivial—a medal, something on the sleeve, a different colored cassock, a handshake—but that withdrawal for a licit cigarette separated the sheep from the goats. Of course the practice in the lower years was to anticipate the privilege, and on Wednesday and Saturday afternoons we younger boys would go off on the county roads to a place called Carrier's where cigarettes and candy could be bought. Ah, to stroll those county roads, smoking, talking, smoking some more. In the spring, when the snow had melted and the fields yielded their fragrance, it was especially wonderful. I can smell the humus still. With time the smoking habit became more demanding, and I would sneak off into the woods near school for a quick smoke. This scofflaw practice had much to do, I have come to believe, with my eventual leaving. (Recently an old classmate, Jim Dech—called of course Poop—sent me a long poem I had written when the smoke shack was pulled down by a new rector in our sixth year. *De lamentatione Rudophi*, which runs five single-spaced pages, is metrically unsure but evocative. I had completely forgotten writing it. Are there other juvenilia destined to come back and haunt me?)

These were the war years, and some of the students would have been in the service if they were not studying for the priesthood. Soon it became obvious that the usual summer vacation, three whole months and more, was inappropriate at the time. And so began what was called Acceleration; my Fourth Year began in the spring of 1945 and would have been completed before the next calendar year if I had stayed. Prefects for the dorms were chosen from Fourth-Year men, and Father Ralph Broker, a painfully ascetic man and another Detacher—his untailored cassock was said to be of the kind altar boys wore—chose me and Bob Lester as prefects of the Second-Year dorm. Shortly after this became known, Mike McDonough, who had preceded me in the job, confronted me on the steps of the Loggia that ran along the front of the school.

"Did Father Broker ask you to be one of his prefects?"

"Yes."

"You're not going to accept, are you?"

Not accept? Being a prefect was one of the plums one had looked forward to.

"Why wouldn't I?"

"Because you're a disgrace to the school. Your whole class is a disgrace."

He went on to catalog our collective faults, and it was the flaunting of the smoking rule that was at the heart of it. Break one rule and it becomes easier to break others. That was his point. How could I honestly exercise a post of authority in the school when I was a notorious breaker of the rule?

I think this was the first time that I saw myself through another's hostile eyes. Yet I agreed with McDonough. I felt awful. But deep inside, I did not really think of myself as other than a model student. I accepted the job despite this chastening experience, but my days at Nazareth Hall were numbered. When summer came, I would leave.

I returned to Nazareth Hall in 1947 after a stint in the Marine Corps, as I have indicated, and was also a college man there, graduating in 1949. Unsurprisingly, however, my most vivid memories are of my first stay there from 1942 to 1945—three years that began in pre-puberty and ended with the thought that celibacy was not for me.

■   The chapel at Nazareth Hall was dedicated to the Annunciation and was a marble marvel, with stained glass windows and embedded stations of the Cross, and it seems now as if no time intervened as I moved with my class, year by year, from the front pews to the back ones where the Sixth-Year men, the temporal lords of the school, knelt. We gathered there each day at noon to recite the Angelus, then filed out in silence to the refectory. After the meal, it was back to chapel again for a brief thanksgiving. And of course our day began there. We rose at six and Mass was at 6:30. By eight o'clock, when classes began, our day was well underway.

In Sixth Year I was elected editor of the *Puer Nazarenus*. If there was any job in that final year I coveted, it was this. The faculty advisor that year was a young priest, Father James Shannon, a man of great charm and talent and energy. Already he was overextended—teaching at Nazareth Hall (Greek and English literature), pursuing graduate studies at the

University of Minnesota, helping out at the cathedral, and other things as well. He came and went in a blur. The first time we talked about the magazine, I sensed his disapproval of its appearance. Ever since I had known it, the *Puer* had been mimeographed, the front cover also drawn on a stencil, the pages then stapled together. I myself had worked with John Murphy in a little room across from the rector's suite, wrapping the stencils around the great drum, then turning the handle with increasing speed as the sheets pulled up. They were wet, of course, and one had to be careful not to smear them. This was labor-intensive but satisfying; one was getting out the *Puer* and had a chance to read *Quid Nunc,* the anonymous humor column, before others saw it. Fred Mertz had written it for several years to great effect. I myself had been *Quid Nunc* for a year. Shannon's reaction to the magazine enabled me to see it for the modest thing it was. But he had a solution. He would look into offset printing, and would himself cover any extra costs. Thus I edited a far more professional-looking magazine than I had inherited, thanks to Father Shannon.

I have home movies of my graduation from Nazareth Hall. Both my grandmothers were there, my Uncle Maurice and Aunt Helen, Aunt Ruth, old friends like Rosie Holl, and my proud parents. And there am I in the black suit and tie I would wear as street clothes when I moved on to the St. Paul Seminary in the fall.

I have used the past tense in speaking of these days, not only because they are past, but because Nazareth Hall is no more. In the madness that succeeded Vatican II, people who had not attended such schools decided that it was wrong to separate boys from their parents at such an early age. These specious arguments prevailed, and Nazareth Hall was sold to Billy Graham for a risible sum. When I go back there now I feel like a recusant wandering through the confiscated churches of England. The baldachino has been removed from the sanctuary, as well as the beautiful altar it covered. On the baldachino had been inscribed the words from Luke 1:34, in Latin, *Spiritus Sanctus superveniet in te, et virtus Altissimi obrumbabit tibi,* and I remember how delighted I was when I found that I could understand them. *The Holy Spirit shall come upon thee, and the power of the Most High will overshadow thee.* The stations are still embedded in the walls, the windows with their Latin too, and oddly the holy water fonts still flank the entry doors. New buildings have been added in the style of the original, which is still called Nazareth Hall, the whole now a part.

Several times I posed on the front steps of the main entrance with my class for photographs. In my first year, Father Connolly, the then rector and the future bishop of Fall River, Massachusetts, chatted there with me and another new boy, Rod Liberati. It was Connolly who, substituting for an absent teacher, wrote "Ratiocination" on the blackboard when it was clear we had not understood. This was not condescension, far from it; we were always addressed as potential peers. On late Saturday afternoons the whole school gathered in the study hall to be addressed by the rector, usually on the history of the archdiocese.

It is a cruel thing to find the setting of so many memories so changed. But it could be in worse hands. Indeed, I marvel at the evangelical accommodation to that papist setting. The statue of the Boy of Nazareth, *Puer Nazarenus*, that stood in the main corridor is gone, but the outdoor statues remain, clinging to their niches—St. Jerome, St. Augustine, St. Thomas Aquinas. Like the iconoclasts of old, those who sold Nazareth Hall have much to answer for. But no later perfidy, on their part or mine, can remove that past from its proper setting, memory.

From time to time I hear from men who were boys with me at Nazareth Hall. All too often, when they tell me what their lives have been, it is a sad story. Some were ordained but left the priesthood; for others it was divorce, estranged children, this or that, and a wistful note comes into their voices when common memories are invoked. Sometimes I think that for those of us who did not go on to the priesthood, Nazareth Hall functions as a kind of Garden of Eden, the measure with reference to which all else must be defective. I have never known anyone from my time there who spoke of the place otherwise than in a laudatory way. Those years formed us and furnished our imagination as well as our memory.

■ The St. Paul Seminary occupied a large tract of land running along the River Road and bordered on one side by the great boulevard Summit Avenue, which runs from the Mississippi into the heart of St. Paul, that is, the cathedral built by Archbishop John Ireland, the great formative spirit of the archdiocese. He also founded St. Thomas College—now in these times of inflationary nomenclature a university—and the major seminary, separated only by Summit. Unlike Nazareth Hall, where everything was contained in one large building, the seminary was a plurality of buildings. What were called Jim Hill's boxcars, the red brick residence halls, did indeed look as if they were mounted on tracks: Grace, Cretin, and Loras. There were also a refectory building cum convent and a classroom building, the second floor of which was the *aula maxima*, where multiclass lectures were given and, on occasion, memorable plays—not least, *Murder in the Cathedral*, in which I was the chorus and Marvin O'Connell played Beckett.

Everything at the major seminary was overtly aimed at our future as priests. First of all, we dressed the role. Our daily garb was a cassock, Roman collar, and biretta. In chapel, wearing surplices over our cassocks, we were ranged in facing choir stalls that filled the whole nave of the place. When we left the grounds—save for an afternoon to St. Thomas across the way, to use the library or gym—we wore black suit and tie and a black hat, covered in winter by a black overcoat. Second, the studies were clearly ecclesiastical: first philosophy, then theology.

The beginning two classes were known as First and Second Philosophers; then there were First, Second, Third, and Fourth Theologians. The target was Holy Orders, the priesthood. First Theologians received the tonsure, making them officially clerics, and then, spread over the next two years of theology, the minor orders were conferred until, at the end of Third Theology, a man was ordained subdeacon. This was the great step. Tonsure might distinguish you from the laity, but the subdiaconate brought with it two things: the promise of celibacy, the better to serve one's bishop and the people, and the obligation to say the office every day. At the beginning of the final year, subdeacons were ordained deacons and then could preach in chapel—we younger seminarians practiced preaching in the refectory, the noise and indifference of the audience enabling us to overcome bashfulness and unease. Such practice sermons seemed addressed to God and the faculty member who taught homiletics, none other than the shy and mumbling Thomas Shanahan, who had moved on from being rector of Nazareth Hall to the post of librarian at the major seminary, where there was a wonderful new library for him to preside over. Deacons could also distribute Holy Communion. Nowadays, when Eucharistic ministers pluck hosts from a ciborium with all the glee of Jack Horner, it is difficult to remember that once to touch the host or indeed the sacred vessels, the chalice and ciborium, was restricted to those with consecrated hands who had promised their lives to God.

The years of philosophy were in effect the junior and senior years of college. At Nazareth Hall I had read a book by Jacques Maritain on aesthetics but, apart from that and my reading in the Prima Pars of the *Summa Theologiae* in my last semester of Latin, I was wholly innocent of philosophy and theology. Now, by contrast with my studies in the major seminary, Nazareth Hall seemed a lovely island of humanities, dominated by what were once called the liberal arts. Here everything was clearly calibrated on a line leading to ordination. At Nazareth Hall, the fact that we were studying for the priesthood was something remote, like being told we would some day be old. It did not play any daily role in our lives. Of course we attended Mass each day, of course we learned Gregorian chant, and Tenebrae was a high moment of the liturgy in the chapel of the Annunciation. The best singers were chosen to sing solo the lamentations: *De lamentatione Jeremiae prophetae. Aleph, Beth,* and so on, ending with *Jerusalem, Jerusalem, convertere ad dominum Deum tuum.* I can still hear those neums dropped into the listening air, the candles extinguished one by one, until the silence was swallowed up in darkness. It was an unforgettable aesthetic, if not religious, moment. But such participation was that of a choir, not the clergy. When Sixth-Year men donned their new black suits at graduation, the garb marked an end and a beginning far more dramatically than the ceremony of graduation. The long years at Nazareth Hall comprised a kind of education that bears only a contingent or, perhaps more accurately, a remote relation to a priestly vocation.

Not so that of the major seminary. It was here that, at a fateful moment, I was introduced to philosophy, taking two courses from a bright and enthusiastic young priest, William Baumgaertner, who had just received his Ph.D. from Laval University. He taught logic and metaphysics by having us read Aristotle's Organon and the *Metaphysics,* with frequent reference to Thomas Aquinas's commentaries. The slogan of Laval could have been, "To the text itself," the text being that of Thomas and of Aristotle. History of Philosophy was taught from a textbook, as was Natural Theology (Butch Baskfield) and Philosophical Psychology (Larry Wolfe), but from the beginning I was taught that it is the primary sources to which one must go. The Latin of Thomas Aquinas was not completely unknown to me, but now it pushed aside the classics. I could not get enough of Aquinas. Father Baumgaertner tutored me in Thomas's commentary on Aristotle's *Nicomachean Ethics.* After First Philosophy, in the summer of 1950, I took the train to Quebec and enrolled in the summer school at Laval. En route, the Korean War broke out, and scanning a Montreal paper I had no idea what or where Corée was.

I will tell of my career as a philosopher later. It was at the seminary that something like a moral schizophrenia set in. During my few years away from seminary life I had dated girls, gone to dances, got a kiss or two. As a seminarian I think I can say I was considered a success as a student. Rudy Bandas, the rector, appointed me chronicler of the seminary and I had to keep a record of passing events of note—not an onerous task but considered an honor. The egg-bald Curly Ryan, our spiritual director, gave us weekly conferences about our vocation. It was impossible not to confront well in advance the great decision one would eventually make. Needless to say, celibacy loomed large. Dating a girl was cause for immediate expulsion. As I had violated the smoking rule at Nazareth Hall, so, at the major seminary I courted disaster with girls. On vacation, Bob McDonald and I would go out on the town as we always had, and we usually ended up with two compliant blondes. Bob, a great wit, would mutter from the back seat from time to time, "Ralph, you shouldn't be here." It was Bob who, when I asked him if he had ever thought of the end of the world, replied, "Which end?" I suppose in a mild way I scandalized him, but we had lots of fun. It was when I was in Second Philosophy that it became clear to me that I was not meant for the priesthood. The prospect of a single life was too much for me.

A classmate of mine had a married sister who lived in veterans' housing on the campus of St. Thomas, just across Summit. As at Nazareth Hall, we had Wednesday and Saturday afternoons free. When my classmate and I dropped by for a visit, another sister was there, from out of town. How did it begin? I don't remember, but begin it did. I began to look forward to those free afternoons because that meant hours of kissing and fondling. And talking about her boyfriend. I had the seminary, she had a boyfriend. It added zest to those stolen hours. The married sister facilitated these meetings, and my classmate seemed to regard the whole thing as a bagatelle. I knew better. I felt divided and miserable. I talked with Curly Ryan and then made an appointment with Bishop Byrne, an auxiliary who was pastor of Nativity parish in St. Paul. He was a severe and rigorous man, and I anticipated hell and brimstone as I told him my story. He was very gentle. He advised me to leave the seminary.

And so, for the second time, not without regret, I left the seminary, armed with my bachelor's degree. I didn't leave it physically right away; at the beginning of summer, I worked at the seminary during the priests' retreat, living in an attic room in Grace and still wearing a cassock and collar. I was visited there by Rich Fleischhaecker, an old classmate from Nazareth Hall with whom I had corresponded while we were both in the service, he in Japan, I in California. In our letters, we had both expressed regret at having left Nazareth Hall and indulged the thought of returning. Restored to civilian life, Rich had lost all intention of becoming a priest. Now, when I told him I was leaving the major seminary, he was very upset. I think he had cast me in the role of sacrificial victim. I would become a priest, and that somehow would justify his living in the world, as we used to say. Well, I felt pretty bad myself.

■ The major seminary was not sold, but it has been cannibalized by St. Thomas University, an institution in ceaseless metastasis. Jim Hill's boxcars are now college dorms. The seminary has been pushed into a corner of the grounds near the chapel. And, my God, the chapel. The choir stalls are gone, and one now enters from the opposite end, where the sanctuary used to be. The place would look like a basketball court if it weren't for the stained glass windows and stations. Such iconoclasm must have been driven by hatred of the sacred. A generation of post-conciliar revolutionaries wreaked havoc on the church. Well, God is merciful. But I find it hard to forgive such sacrilege.

PATERFAMILIAS

SOME YEARS AGO, WHENEVER I WAS DRIVING A FAIR DISTANCE, I BEGAN
the habit of going down the list of our children and seeing how many
things I could remember of each of them. I proceed chronologically:
Cathy, Mary, Anne, Dave, Beth, and Dan. Of course that is not the whole
story. Our first child, Michael, died when he was three. Some of his brothers and sisters never knew him. No matter. One day they will. He lies now
beside Connie in Cedar Grove, and I will lie there with them bye and bye.

■ Connie and I were in the fiftieth year of our marriage when she died
on May 18, 2002. By then all our children were married and gone, raising
families of their own, and we had moved to a house in the northern sub-
urb of Granger, something we had once vowed never to do. For thirty-
three years we lived at 2158 Portage Avenue in South Bend, in a great brick
house on an acre and a half of lawn. Only our youngest, Daniel, was born
after we moved there, but all the children grew up in that house and I am
sure it is the place that figures in their earliest memories.

Connie and I were introduced one fateful Saturday in April, 1952, when
I was at my typewriter at the Catholic Youth Center on Park Avenue in

Minneapolis, preparing an issue of the little magazine I edited for Father Baglio, the director of the center and my part-time employer. I was doing graduate work at the University of Minnesota in philosophy, but every day I put in several hours at the center. In the manner of celibates, Baglio was a tireless matchmaker, and on this occasion he looked in at me, all smiles. "There's someone you've got to meet."

The someone was Constance Terrill Kunert, who had come to the CYC in the improbable role of assistant leader of a troop of girl scouts. We met in the pool room in the basement because that is where their tour of the center had reached. She was of medium height, her black hair worn in what was called a pageboy, with a lovely smile that had a nice sardonic edge to it. That might have been it if I hadn't run into her on campus some days later. She was completing her junior year. We went off to the Bridge Café for coffee and I met some of her friends. We went out, I introduced her to Bob McDonald. I met her parents, I brought her home. In a memory book she prepared for a granddaughter, Connie wrote that I began to talk marriage right from the beginning. I can believe it. I had gone with half a dozen girls since returning to the world, I had brought some of them home, I had sensed the lack of enthusiasm in my mother. My father had been impressed by one Catherine Brown. But both my parents took to Connie immediately, as who would not have?

I have sometimes thought that our marriage was such a good one because we scarcely knew one another on our wedding day. We met in April, when I was in the throes of completing my master's dissertation, defending it, finishing the spring quarter, and working at the CYC. I wanted to get my M.A. in one year so that in the fall I could continue my graduate work in Quebec. The quarter ended early in June, and I went off to Baraboo, Wisconsin, with my family to work at the powder plant where my father was project engineer—that's powder in the sense of gunpowder—and live on the shore of Lake Delton. On Friday night I roared off in a car pool to Minneapolis, a drive of over three hundred miles, in order to be with Connie. As often as not, we spent time with my brother Roger and his wife Lue, who had an apartment overlooking Loring Park. Did I go up every weekend? I think I did. But one week Connie spent with my family at Lake Delton. Then, early in September 1952, I went off to Quebec to begin my studies at Université Laval. The plan was that I would return after the fall semester, and Connie and I would marry so I could bring her back to Quebec with me. We were married on January 3, 1953, in her parish church of St. Thomas the Apostle, Father Cleary presiding. Bob McDonald was my best man, and in the sanctuary were Fathers Baumgaertner and Henri DuLac, both graduates of Laval and both regarding me as a protégé. (The previous summer, I had wisely decided against accepting an offer from Father DuLac to teach at St. Thomas on the basis of my M.A.) Connie and I spent our first night at the Lowell Inn in Stillwater, Minnesota, then drove back to Minneapolis the next morning to catch the train to Quebec. We had an upper in the Pullman car and in the morning, when we parted the curtains and looked out, we found that all the other berths had been stashed away and the seats were filled with black-suited seminarians returning to Windsor. We arrived in Quebec on the Epiphany, January 6. It was a town made even more charming by newly fallen snow, lots of it. We were, in a sense, home.

One could calculate how many hours and days Connie and I were actually together before our wedding, but if either of us had been calculating we probably would have waited. During the fall, Connie had foregone her senior year of college in order to work in a boutique to raise money for our future life. To this day I can scarcely believe my own economic naiveté. I had exhausted the G. I. Bill by this point, and a non-Canadian could not get a fellowship at Laval. I had made some money working in Baraboo, but during the fall semester in Quebec I was living on fifteen dollars a week sent by my mother, a week at a time. Five dollars went for my room, so I had the grand total of ten dollars to live on. Breakfast—coffee and toast—cost fifteen cents. I could get a dinner special for sixty-three cents, and have lunch for a quarter at the Greek restaurant across from the Faculté de philosophie on the Chemin Ste-Foye. That adds up to something like $7.25 a week for meals. I was thin but healthy.

After our marriage, the parental dole increased to $150 a month, half of which went for rent. At first we shared an apartment with a grass widow named Yolande and then with a divorced man, Ross Thilman, who was seldom home. Next we moved into a basement apartment at 60 Avenue des Braves. In December, Michael was born at Hôpital St. Sacrement, on a Sunday. The Germains, in whose house we were living, took us off to the hospital early in the morning. In the manner of those sensible days, I was kept away from the proceedings. Labor went on all day but finally the news came. *Puer natus est nobis.* They let me see Connie and then I went off with George Lavere to celebrate, the two of us singing a then popular song, "O Mine Papa."

How in the world we managed to afford a child on our budget I don't remember. But then, that was a feature of our life together. Connie was the practical one, so she became chancellor of the exchequer. This was meant to free me for my work. I came to Quebec with an M.A. In the summer of 1953 I was given a Licence en philosophie, magna cum laude; my doctorate, summa cum laude, was awarded in the spring of 1954. But we had already left in April, my folks having come to take the three of us to Silver Bay above Duluth, where my father was now project manager of the taconite plant. Connie's folks drove up to fetch us a few weeks later and take us back to their home in Minneapolis. I myself had idiotically agreed to return to Quebec to teach summer school English. I suppose I was flattered to be asked. Connie kept the daily letters I wrote her, and after her death I found one of them in the table beside her bed. Why she had put that one there, I cannot say. I pored over it for significance, but it was only the lovesick letter of an absent husband. In the fall we would be heading for Omaha, where I would begin teaching philosophy at the Jesuit university, Creighton. The salary was $3,700 for nine months.

Perhaps everyone remembers the addresses at which he has lived. In Omaha we lived in a row house at 4111 Valley, with two floors. My brother Rog and Bob McDonald pulled a trailer load of inherited furniture from Minneapolis for us. My father gave us his 1949 Hudson, on which he had put a lot of miles, but it was only five years old. The camshaft had a disconcerting way of sliding forward when you braked; it was turtle-shaped and had a miniature shifting device beneath the steering wheel, not the usual stick. Living above ground for a change, surrounded by other young couples, we were a family. Our friends were for the most part connected to Creighton, but already Connie showed her knack for making friends and soon knew everyone living around us.

In December I received a letter from the University of Notre Dame, telling me that my job would be ready the following fall. This was and was not a surprise. Charles De Koninck, dean of the Faculté de Philosophie at Laval, director of my dissertation, and all I hoped to become, had told me that he wanted me to teach at Notre Dame. Other students of his were already there. He wrote Notre Dame and was told, not this year but next. Sure. By that time I had become acquainted with the hard cold facts about academic employment. I had sent out some fifty letters to departments of philosophy announcing my availability. Most of them went unanswered. In the end I received two offers, one from Villanova University, which in-

volved classics and philosophy, and the other from Creighton, where I
went to be interviewed shortly after we had arrived at the Kunerts' home.
Ed Rousseau has told me that I had clinched the job halfway into the interview, having allayed his fears about having a Laval Thomist of the strict
observance on the faculty. Connie and I loved Creighton, we had made
friends, I was flourishing, but still, it was Notre Dame. When I told the
dean at Creighton that I would not be back in the fall, he was unhappy.
Years later I would learn that he had actually written to his counterpart at
Notre Dame, objecting to this raiding of his faculty. All this gave me an
undeserved luster when I arrived in South Bend.

We had four addresses in South Bend. Our first year, 1955–56, we
were at 1727 S. Michigan, a house that no longer exists. We then moved
to 15A Vetville, also long since demolished, then to 3317 Rexford Drive,
from which we moved to our house on Portage Avenue.

Marriage is the school in which most of us learn our own defects as
well as the joys and griefs of life. I have a vivid memory of the moment
in Quebec when I realized that Connie was an autonomous person, not
just a footnote to my life. That realization presented the chance, at least,
to emerge from egoism. With the birth of Michael, then of Cathleen in
September of 1955, and of Mary in September 1956, the hectic and demanding but deeply satisfying task of raising children was thrust upon
us. Connie was to have seven children in the course of some ten and a half
years. We just had them. That was the point of being married. And in
those days seven was not considered a large number of children, among
Catholics, I mean.

We had moved into 15A Vetville in 1956 because it was cheaper and we
were facing the prospect of large medical bills. The rent was thirty-five
dollars a month. Only a few units were reserved for faculty. Those fertile
acres, with their rows of barrack-like buildings, children all over the place,
were meant for married students. Our living there as the family of a faculty member was a concession, though it was difficult to think of it as a
prize. The village is long gone, of course, commemorated by a plaque. I can
locate the exact spot where 15A stood, directly west from the north corner formed by the meeting of Bulla and Juniper. Before we could make
the move from Michigan Avenue, Connie was off to the hospital to have
Mary: she went from one address, and I brought her home to another. So
now there were five of us, Connie and I, Michael, Cathy, and Mary. The
months ahead were to be our via dolorosa. We were on the threshold of

the first great tragedy of our lives. There is a photograph of me at that time, seated on the sofa, bracketed by Mary and Cathy. My expression is one of both joy and sorrow.

Already in Omaha, Michael's doctor had expressed concern about him, and we went to South Bend with his recommendation of a pediatrician. The diagnosis eventually was encephalitis, perhaps due to the mumps Connie had contracted during her pregnancy. Throughout our first year in South Bend the concern had mounted, and in the summer of 1956 Michael went into the hospital for his first operation. The idea was to introduce a tube to relieve the pressure on his brain. I think there were three such attempts, all eventually unsuccessful. He spent time in every hospital in South Bend: Childrens', Memorial, St. Joseph. He died on a Sunday, February 10, 1957, not two months after his third birthday. We learned the meaning of loss.

Michael was buried in Highland Cemetery on Portage Avenue, in a row reserved for children. It was February, snow lay on the ground, and we all followed the priests from the cars parked along the cemetery road, Connie and I coming in a car supplied by McGann, the funeral director. Our parents were there, making the long trip from Minneapolis to bury their first grandchild. Our friends the Oesterles were there, the Fitzgeralds, the Smiths, the Caponigris, the Bobiks, and other colleagues, many of them now long since dead themselves.

When Michael was buried our stay in South Bend was also sealed as permanent. We could not have left him and gone elsewhere, not permanently. And his loss confirmed as well my allegiance to Notre Dame. In 1963 we bought the house on Portage Avenue, a short walk from Highland Cemetery, and for years I would go out there to Michael's grave and grieve the loss of our firstborn. I could see his grave from the road when I drove past. In 1999 we moved him from Highland Cemetery to Cedar Grove, where we had bought three plots. Our friend, Father Marvin O'Connell conducted the brief ceremony.

■ One survives such experiences because they retain a note of the incredible. When it was over, Father Philip Moore, vice president of Academic Affairs, called me in. He had a Popeye jaw and a gruff manner, but he too was a philosopher, and I had always found him kind. He mumbled something about the trouble we'd been through, then told me to make a list of what we owed and give it to him. The university would take care of everything. What was more, we would be given a down payment on a house so we could have our own place. Those were simpler days. A neophyte like myself knew and was known by the officers of the university. Father Hesburgh would have put on sackcloth and ashes if he ran into a member of the faculty he didn't know.

Things have changed, as things will. The Ladies of Notre Dame once consisted of the wives of professors, and at his annual dinner for the faculty, Father Hesburgh would acknowledge the role that wives played in the work of Notre Dame, subsidiary, of course, as helpmates to their husbands. In those days there wasn't a wife who objected to that. Hesburgh was incapable of a social gaffe or of offending an audience. Well, not wholly incapable. Once, speaking at length after one of his dinners for the faculty, he came to the end of what he had to say—usually a travelogue to divert us homebodies with an account of where he had been during the year—and looked out over the tables on each of which was a floral arrangement. He said it would be a shame to just leave them, but how to fairly distribute them? Then came the epiphany: "I have it. The oldest woman at each table take the flowers." Well, on that basis the flowers would still be rotting in the dining hall like Miss Haversham's wedding cake.

The kind of help we were given by the university would come to be regarded as paternalistic. Perhaps it was. But when you're down and out, a parent is what you need. I recently found a letter from the nun who directed St. Joseph Hospital, in which she wiped out anything we owed beyond what was covered by Blue Cross. I was only in my second year at Notre Dame when this happened, but the university response did not wholly surprise me. Of course, helping us buy a house was to help us put down roots. I had come to Notre Dame as to the promised land and from the beginning had felt welcomed into what was unabashedly called the Notre Dame family. Of course, it would be ironic now to apply such a phrase to a faculty who are largely strangers to one another, but in those years it was a justifiably analogous use of "family"—as I would have pedantically put it.

Eventually, all six of our surviving children graduated from Notre Dame, and the Basilica of the Sacred Heart, the campus church, would be the setting of baptisms, weddings, funerals. Michael was buried from there, and it was there on a chill spring day, May 21, 2002, that Connie's funeral Mass was said and Father Marvin O'Connell, who had become almost one of the family, preached a memorable homily.

When Connie's cancer was first diagnosed, I called my friend Dr. Alex Shyrger at the Mayo Clinic and he urged me to bring her there. Lou Solomon came along and stayed in Rochester for the time it took to confirm the seriousness of Connie's illness. Dave and Lou Solomon had long been our closest friends on the faculty; never had friendship meant more than during the following seven months.

As I followed the casket down the aisle, accompanied by my children and their spouses, the sense of being an emotional amputee was softened by their presence. They have all of them married wonderfully well, they all have families of their own, and they had taken turns to be with their mother in her last months. Our friend Sally Norton had come from Devon to spend two weeks with Connie in April and helped her decide which of the girls would get which items of jewelry. And they had spent an afternoon rearranging in its cabinet the bone china Connie had been given by her grandmother. Once Connie and I had followed Michael's little white casket down that same aisle, and now I was following hers. We walked to the cemetery up Notre Dame Avenue, and after the burial and a luncheon for the hundreds who had come to the funeral, I went home with my children. Anne stayed with me for several days, but then I was alone in an empty house. It was days before I could even weep.

■ I had been appointed to the President's Committee on Arts and Humanities in 2001 but could not attend the first meeting because of Connie's illness. When I suggested that if I did go, Mary, who lived in Baltimore, could come along, Connie sat up, eyes flashing, "Don't you dare." The suggestion brought home that we were waiting for her death, and her feisty response was meant to push away the realization. Not that she had any illusions about her condition. We had once promised that we would never keep medical news from one another, and I had the awful duty of telling her when the doctors said there was no need of further treatment. For one MRI, I took her to St. Joseph Hospital, where she stayed overnight. I found a priest for her and when he came, Sally was in the room. He asked Connie if she would like to receive communion. She looked at him. "I think I'll go to confession first." Sally and I stepped into the hall. After that, Connie was fully resigned to what lay ahead. Father John Jenkins brought her communion at home, and Father Ernan McMullin, a veritable hero of the works of mercy (when Michael was dying, he was often there with us), visited as well. Connie had a final luncheon party for her women friends, Nancy Kommers, Liz Christman, Carole McKim, Pat Weber, Nan Shane, Lou Solomon—each of whom seemed sure she was her closest and dearest friend, and it went off well.

One or the other of my daughters has usually accompanied me to Washington for meetings of the President's Committee, since there are social functions involved, and they have had a chance to meet Laura Bush. Recently both Anne and Mary came with me, and afterward we drove to Baltimore, Mary at the wheel, Anne beside her, me in the back. My daughters have grown into beautiful women and it takes great discipline not to blurt out to others how I love and admire them and my sons. On that occasion, listening to my daughters chattering in the front seat, I was all but overwhelmed with pride in them. All the children bear the impress of their mother, though in different ways. Doubtless that is why we have been spared the heartbreak that comes when one's child drifts away, going down paths of which one cannot approve, freaking out one way or another. If this does not happen, it is a blessing, not an accomplishment of the parents, save in small part. And that part, I believe, is largely due to the mother. In the grammar from which I learned Latin there was an illustration of a Roman matron, the famous Cornelia, with her children. When a wealthy friend spoke of her jewels, Cornelia said, pointing to her sons, *Haec sunt margaritae meae.* These are my jewels. I loved to give Connie rings and watches and bracelets and earrings and necklaces. They have all been distributed now to her real jewels.

FIVE

EUROPE

Louvain

One September day in 1959 we set out on our first trip to Europe. We sailed from Hoboken on the *Statendam,* bound for Southampton and on to Amsterdam, courtesy of the Fulbright Commission. I had been awarded a research scholarship to Belgium, to Louvain University for the academic year. By the terms of the grant, Fulbright paid the travel expenses of the scholar alone, though the stipend in Belgium was predicated on our number. I had been awarded a Belgian-American Fellowship as well as the Fulbright, could not have accepted both, and chose the Fulbright because it amounted to a lot more support. But the travel expenses for Connie and three children—Anne had arrived the previous October—presented an obstacle. When I was discussing my good fortune with Father Sheedy, the dean of the College of Arts and Letters, the matter of passage for my family came up. He dismissed it as only one who has taken the vow of poverty could. "We'll take care of that." And they did, so there we were in first class, the children looked after by a nanny, rubbing shoulders with the affluent and not wholly comfortable. From time to time we would slip down to whatever the next class was called, and there we met other Fulbright awardees. Why weren't they in first class? I realized that in the pecking order of the foundation, a research scholar outranked someone like Ray Lavallee, who would be teaching in Dinant, and Ernie Trumble, who would be teaching in Liège, to say nothing of mere graduate students like Jeffrey Russell. None of this mattered once we were in Belgium, and we became quite close to the Lavallees and the Trumbles, the former from Iowa, the latter from Oklahoma. Connie's twenty-eighth birthday occurred while we were aboard, on September 25, 1959, and a great fuss was made about it in the dining room. Violinists came to our table, a special cake was brought in, Connie was asked what music she would like to hear. I was delighted by all this but, like Connie, was not wholly comfortable in those surroundings. Professors in those days knew the meaning of penury.

Since I had entertained fantasies about Europe from reading about the expatriate American authors, I was glad to be going at last. Yet at the same time I felt impossibly old, a late bloomer, as one might have said, though it sounds like expired underwear. All my heroes had been off to Europe in their twenties—some earlier, if they had been in World War I—and here I was, at the advanced age of thirty, making my first crossing. But of course I was traveling in my guise as philosopher, the grant was to enable me to study the relationship between Heidegger and Aristotle, and fiction was not in prospect.

Connie had been given a lot of bad advice on how to survive a year in Europe with a family. Just about everything she was told turned out to be false. In one trunk we had actually packed cooking utensils, as if these would be unknown in Belgium. Connie was given stories about the impossibility of doing laundry, of the hazards of shopping, all of them utterly false. It was an extremely pleasant year. After the orientation in Brussels, we rented the apartment of a Dr. Zimmerman, who was off to Philadelphia for the year. The apartment was located one floor from the top of the Atlantic Building, on the Avenue des Alliés (Bondgenotenlaan) just before it runs into the Place Foch. It was beautifully furnished, the concierge became Connie's protectress, and we had a cleaning lady. Whatever the stipend, it enabled us to live better than we ever had before. I actually bought a new car, a Citroen à deux chevaux, in which we traveled everywhere, and when I sold it at the end of the year, I got seven hundred dollars for it. It had cost about nine hundred new. It was the first year that Connie ran our household without anxiety about money.

Cathy had just turned four, Mary was just three, and Anne was not yet a year old. We were made welcome by Belgians who had spent time in the States on reverse Fulbrights, and on their advice we decided to enroll Cathy and Mary in the preschool at the Soeurs de Marie. This was to furnish the germ for my first published story, "The First Farewell." They soon loved it. Each morning I would set out for the Institut de Philosophie with the girls in tow, drop them at their school, and then go on to the Institute. This was founded by Cardinal Mercier, one of the great figures in the Thomistic Revival inaugurated by Leo XIII's 1879 encyclical *Aeterni Patris*. The then director was Father Louis De Raymaecker, and he formally received me in his office, gave me tea, and politely inquired about my work, my colleagues, my university. In that setting I felt that I was being initiated into the sources of my philosophical outlook (Charles De Koninck held his doctorate from Louvain). Years later, in the early 1980s, I was a visiting professor at the University of Leuven, lecturing in English, and one day I went to pay my respects to the current director. Making conversation, I said something to the effect that it must be extremely satisfying to occupy that office, given the enormous influence of the institute. He raised a hand to stop me. "We don't do that sort of thing anymore." Ah yes. Even the great centers of Thomism had abandoned their patrimony.

Although my main task was my own research, I also took part in the De Wulf Mansion Seminar with Suzanne Mansion—the niece of the great Auguste—and with Gerald Verbeke, Jean Ladrière, others. But for the most part I was at work in the institute library or in the main library located on Hoover Platz. Often in the afternoon I would write at the dining-room table in our apartment, from whose windows we had an unequaled view of the library tower. Far more dramatically than any clock, the tower told the time of day by the play of the weather on it and the dramatic sunsets that silhouetted it against the evening sky. Of course it had a chiming clock as well—a good thing, since Belgium is not noted for its sun. It was at that dining-room table that I wrote my first book, but more of that anon.

We were determined to take maximum advantage of our year and see as much as we could. We made several excursions into Holland, riding the canals of Amsterdam and visiting the miniature town of Meduridam. And of course to Antwerp, to Dinant to visit Ray and Felicia Lavallee, to Bruges, and to Ghent. We invaded Germany and were robbed in Cologne of cameras and some dolls of the girls. The Citroen had a top that was little more than a window shade; this had been cut through and the items plucked from the back seat. Ah well. Germans. We went on to Bonn and continued east, visiting Dachau. At Christmas we traveled to Davos in Switzerland, to St. Josef Haus, a former hospital, where I fell ill, feeling like Hans Castorp. The nuns plied me with hot milk into which eggs had been stirred, a Dominican gave me a German work on existentialism when he heard what my research project was, and I lay reading while Connie and the kids cavorted in the winter paradise. One night Connie went on a sleigh ride with a group of seminarians, an ambiguous excursion she never failed to refer to without a sly look. I could make the look fade by reminding her that she had married a former seminarian.

At Easter we drove to Paris, which was of course crowded, and we had a difficult time getting settled. My besetting sin as a traveler is never to make plans in advance, but rather to drive into a town in the full expectation that comfortable accommodations can be had. By and large this is true, but in Europe in those days, and on holidays, it was not. One of the places where I stopped to see if they could accommodate us turned out to be a brothel. We were not flying completely blind. We had met and regularly entertained a number of American priests studying at Louvain. There were several from Kentucky; Jim Doig from Notre Dame; Dave Boileau, a Michiganer from the diocese of Little Rock; Bob Smith of Rockville Center; and Tony Lovegrove of Hove, who rode a motorcycle with RAF abandon. The map of Europe for these men consisted of religious houses or inexpensive hotels where they could stay when they were traveling. It was from them that we had learned of St. Josef Haus in Davos, and Connie actually arranged for our stay there before we left Louvain. These more or less short excursions went on throughout the year, but in the spring we set off on our grand tour. We went down the Rhine valley, over to Switzerland, and then through the Brenner Pass to Italy and on to Rome; in returning, we followed the Riviera and went west to Spain and Barcelona, after which we ascended through France to Paris and then home to Louvain.

Connie kept a book in which she logged our progress and recorded our expenses. There were five of us, two adults, three children, and an automobile that however abstemious did need gas from time to time. We made the great circuit I have sketched on less than a thousand dollars, closer to eight hundred dollars. We were not traveling first class, but only rarely did we stop at a place we wished to flee as soon as possible. Germany was less hospitable to children, to put it mildly, whereas in Italy the sight of our little girls was the open sesame. In Florence a waiter took Anne and led her up and down so that everyone at the outside tables could see her. Anne had been a babe in arms when we left home, and I remember the joy with which we abandoned her stroller in Heidelberg. From now on she could walk or at least be carried. The front wheel of the stroller was possessed by a demon who made forward progress all but impossible. In parting with it, I effectively told the demon to take it home with him.

In Louvain, French was the language of the university and shops, but beneath the surface the resentment of the Flemish toward the French-speaking Walloons seethed. The time would come when prosperity switched from the Walloons to the Flemings, and the latter made their move. The impact on the university was almost comic. The historic university would become Flemish—Leuven—and a new university would be built for the French-speaking students, not directly reachable from the old, called Université Catholique de Louvain. My dear friend Eugeen DeJonghe was then an officer of the university and argued fruitlessly against this division. How do you divide a historic library? "Eenie meenie minie mo" was the method agreed on, one for you, one for me. Well, the havoc this wrought has been somewhat repaired by time, but the prestige and influence of the university have been halved by this doubling.

That year Connie went on a trip to Libya with Felicia Lavallee, who had a sister in Tripoli. I, in turn, drove to Copenhagen in order to present offprints of articles I had written on Kierkegaard to the Royal Library. On the way back I stopped at the University of Groningen to see if I could find a copy of G. L. Muskens's book on analogy, which had been a dissertation there. Coming through Breda, passing a hospital, I was hit broadside by a car that came roaring out of the drive. My little car tumbled over, I was thrown out, and the car came to rest on my inner leg. I was briefly in shock, but then I looked up into the face of a bearded Capuchin and thought it was all over. *Nunc dimittis.* I was taken into the hospital and checked over. Nothing broken. The damage had been to my clothing and my car. Connie was notified and was driven up by a contingent of our clerical friends. When she came into the ward, the way I lay gave her the impression that I had lost a leg. After that shock wore off, she and her cohorts seemed almost disappointed that I was not on the brink of death or maimed for life. They had to settle for the bad news about the car.

The car was repaired for a negligible sum, and I later went up to Breda to retrieve it. I was clearly the innocent party in the accident, as the other driver, the wife of a physician, had insisted as she followed me into the hospital. Her memory altered under the counsel of calculating friends. After all, I was an American and therefore presumably rich. For years I was annoyed by official letters demanding that I appear in court in Breda to answer the charges against me. Replies more appropriate to my time in the Marines than to a professor of philosophy occurred, but I simply ignored these absurd demands and eventually they stopped.

■ When our year was done and the car sold, we headed for England. We visited Tony Lovegrove's family and had a picnic at Norfolk, then on to London. We stayed near Victoria station in a bed and breakfast, and the kids loved the breakfasts, as big as those in Holland. We went sightseeing by public transportation—the Abbey, the Tower, Oxford Street. Now when I see young couples traveling with their children I find it difficult to believe the insouciance with which we set off with our three little ones, doing things we ourselves had never done before. Only the young have the resilience for such adventures. In Rome I can locate the hotel in which we stayed, having arrived unannounced. I simply drove around stopping at hotels and asking if they could put us up. The Olympics were about to be held in Rome, and this complicated matters so far as housing went. We ended up in a place not far from the Piazza San Silvestro, on the top floor, in one room with one large bed for the five of us. Am I wrong to think we managed it because it all seemed a game, unreal, fun? In Rome I drove up to the front steps of St. Peter's on a Wednesday, and we went in to see Pope John XXIII being carried into the basilica, blessing benignly as the carriers struggled under his avoirdupois. It was pure chance, but at the time it seemed just right. You want to see the Pope? Drop into St. Peter's. As if he were perpetually on display. Connie had her hair done on the Corso, and I have a wonderful photograph of her in her new French roll, with one of the fountains in St. Peter's square as background. She is beautiful, the woman I loved. Whenever I pass that fountain I think of that photograph and of late would like to cry, except that the memory is so pleasant. That trip was the harbinger of two more pleasant years in Rome.

In London the kids came down with mumps and we had to smuggle them aboard and into the cabin before anyone noticed. Once underway, we called the ship's doctor, and they received wonderful care and arrived cured. Our next voyage by ship would exact revenge for this ruse.

Oxford, Edinburgh, Duns

My next European trip, in 1965, was solo. I flew to Britain for a Dun Scotus meeting that began in Oxford, went on to Edinburgh, and ended with the unveiling of a memorial to the Subtle Doctor at Duns. I lodged in Merton College and was most impressed by the original library, with its warped wavy floors and sections named after the liberal arts. The post-Reformation shenanigans at high table stood in stark contrast to the origins of the college and the university. It is only in recent years, with Eamon Duffy's *Stripping of the Altars,* that the English have been made to confront the depredations of Henry and Elizabeth. This is likely due to the fact that nowadays belief of any kind is in short supply in once Merrie England. What was I, a Thomist, doing at a Scotus conference? Reading a paper, of course, on Scotus and univocity and enjoying the Franciscan triumphalism of the occasion. In Oxford I had tea with Stephen Brown and the bishop of Beirut—or was he only one of the bishops of Beirut?—and in Edinburgh, at a reception given by the provost of the city, there was a Trappist abbot wearing a swallow-tail coat and a hearing aid. Think about it.

Via Ugo Balzani

The *annus mirabilis* of our family has to be 1969–70, which we spent in Rome courtesy of the National Endowment for the Humanities. The year began with a series of disasters. Mindful of our pleasant Fulbright voyage, we planned to travel by ship. I had flown to the Scotus meeting, and being set down in England after a few hours in the air seemed too abrupt. There were now eight in our party, with David and Beth and Dan having come along in 1961, 1962, and 1964, respectively. The ship was to embark from a Manhattan dock, so there was no need, as before, to arrange for transfer to Hoboken. We settled into a hotel within sight of the ship, and Dave and I went off to drop something at my then literary agent's, walking most of the way. The following day we went aboard, all the wonderful memories of the *Statendam* came back, the kids loved it, and we weighed anchor and were off. As the ship progressed up the east coast, Beth fell ill. Seasickness? Perhaps. The nurse and doctor visited her. She didn't get better. The pain was severe in her abdomen. It turned out to be appendicitis. What to do? There was an operating theater on board, but this was for emergency purposes. Nor did the ship's doctor look eager to perform surgery. The solution was to disembark at Halifax so that Beth could be operated on there. There was talk of sending out a helicopter, but that was not necessary. We docked, an ambulance was waiting, and we all followed Beth to the hospital.

There was a ten-day recovery period after the operation. Our ship sailed away. The first night we all, all but Beth, stayed in a reception depot for immigrants. It was an experience that induced long thoughts of my ancestors during the night. All our plans had collapsed. The VW van that awaited us in Le Havre would wait in vain. The boat tickets had been given back to me, so I guess we sailed from New York to Halifax for free. To our rescue came a marvelous doctor and his family, who helped us get settled in a rooming house and entertained us at their home. The kids loved it. Meanwhile, I had to figure out how to get us to Rome. The original idea was to pick up our van and drive in a leisurely fashion to Italy. I was able to exchange the ship tickets for air fare to Montreal and then to Paris. The plan was that from Paris I would then go to Le Havre, pick up the van, return for the family, and drive us all to Rome. The problem was that the papers that had been prepared for the van were now out of date, and new ones would not be ready for a week. So there we were stranded in Paris. We did a little sightseeing; we ran into John Beach and his wife, just returning from their place on the Costa Brava (a philosopher with a place on the Spanish Riviera?); and we fretted. My solution was to take all the traveler's checks that had been meant to make our journey to Rome so pleasant and buy plane tickets to Rome. Eight tickets pretty well wiped us out, but we had to get to Rome.

We got to Rome. Father Mullahy, who had spent years in Rome at the generalate of the Congregation of Holy Cross, had assured me that Vince McAloon would smooth our way, help get us settled, and find a place for us to spend the year. I was ready to be pampered. We called on Vince in his ad hoc Notre Dame Club near Santa Maria Maggiore and, more importantly, near the restaurant the Scoglio di Frisio. Vince had graduated from Notre Dame in the late 1930s and spent the war years in Italy. He never went home. (Well, eventually he did. He returned to campus and lived with the brothers in Columba Hall until he died.) He was the soul of affability and Irish charm. He was a big hit with the kids. He was utterly useless. His way of helping us find an apartment was to give me a copy of the ads in *Il Tempo*. I went to an agency, was taken to an apartment at Via Ugo Balzani 6, and rented it. I would have rented any apartment I was taken to first. Then I rented a car, we had our gear delivered to the apartment, and we moved in. The next step was getting the children enrolled at Marymount. This was all arranged, but of course we had shown up later than planned. I had rented the smallest and cheapest Fiat, and the eight of us got into it like Keystone Kops and drove out to the Cassia Antica and Marymount. Cathy would start high school there, while Mary, Anne, Dave, and Beth were still in the lower grades. The reception could not have been warmer.

The next step was to fly back to Paris and take the train to Le Havre to pick up our VW van. David came into the front hall of the apartment where I was saying goodbye to Connie and trying to act as if the past couple of weeks were no indication of what lay ahead. When I opened the door to go, I turned and looked down at Dave. His eyes were wide, his mouth half open, he might have been taking a final look at me. It nearly broke my heart to leave them. Connie could cope with anything, but I felt I was abandoning them. At the airport I found that the first plane to Paris did not leave until the following morning. Return to the apartment? I could not face another such farewell. So I dozed in Fiumicino until morning, then flew to Paris. I got to Le Havre by train and with minimum fuss and red tape took possession of the van.

I had never driven such a vehicle before. I learned how on the drive to Paris, drove right through the city, sailing around some roundabouts several times to get oriented, and soon was on my way south. I drove from Le Havre to Rome in one burst, something like twenty-hours. The tunnels and bridges had not yet straightened out the coastal roads on the Riviera, so negotiating that part of the trip required alertness. I stopped and napped for an hour and then got under way again, anxious to get back to the apartment and Connie and the kids. I made it. When I drove in, they all came down to look at the vehicle in which we would travel so many miles, and which, unlike those I had just covered, we could enjoy.

A year that began in that way might have given us a pause. It did. But we were young. I was forty, Connie had not yet turned thirty-eight. The older girls were little mothers and had a Connie-like way of managing their younger siblings. The fact was that all the disasters that were to happen had already happened. From that point on, the year was the best we had yet spent, both as a family and individually. The kids still talk about it. Cathy told me a year ago that, having found the Marymount website, she sent them a message telling them that her year with them had changed her life. Mary visited Rome again when she spent her college sophomore year in Innsbruck; Dave honeymooned there, to show Nancy the scenes of his youth, and they have spent longer periods in Rome with their three children. Anne was there as an architecture student.

The five older children were settled at Marymount, so what about Danny? He had just turned five. Where did we hear of Mrs. Trujillo and her school on the Monte Parioli? We did, we enrolled Danny, and thanks to that we met Sally Norton. She and Connie were to become dear friends. Sally and Guy Norton entertained us all at their country place, Abadia Celestina, any number of times and in later years often visited us in the States. The Nortons were expatriate Englishmen; Guy owned a tobacco company, Deltafina. Their son Alexander was a classmate of Danny's in the preschool. That was the occasion for what was to become one of our longest and more enduring friendships. The Nortons have returned to England now and are settled in Stoke Gabriel in Devon, where I visit them from time to time.

All of our children were in school. This would drain our savings, but I could always replenish them with fiction. We had the whole day to ourselves. I rented a typewriter and spent the morning writing the novel that would be called *The Priest*. (Its working title was *Where No Storms Come*, a lovely line from Hopkins, but it sounded like a soap opera.) My idea was that I would get it drafted and then turn to the philosophical research for which I had come. And that is more or less how it turned out. After I had finished my morning writing stint, off we would go to Trastevere or to one of the restaurants tucked away on the streets that move off from the Piazza di Spagna. I seem to have the most vivid memories of the Otello, and of Sabatini's in Trastevere. We are at an outside table, the food is wonderful, the weather is wonderful, a musician comes along, stops, screws his flute together, and begins to play. Cats wind between our ankles. "This is why we fought the war," I explain to Connie.

When I had finished the draft of my novel, I wound down by writing a quickie that would be published as *Spinnaker*. Then I signed in at the Vatican Library, got my ID, and with some regularity worked there in the mornings. Afterward Connie and I would meet and have our leisurely lunch in one of the many restaurants around the Vatican. What was I working on? Boethius.

We made the reverse of our 1960 grand tour that year, driving from Rome up through Paris and into Belgium. Did the girls remember Louvain? Somewhat. We went to Barcelona again, staying once more at the Hotel Havana. In Perpignan it rained and rained. We went to Greece, too, driving to Bari and taking a ferry which stopped at Corfu and went on the next day to Greece. The boat was the *Egnetia*. We drove to Athens, we drove around the Peloponnese. Photographs of the kids scrambling around the Parthenon bring those days back so vividly. And there is Connie in a black pants-suit, edged with red, her hair still artfully dark, looking as young as her daughters. It was a feature of that year that even while it was going on, we all knew it to be the best year of our life as a family.

Via Aurelia

We returned to Rome for the 1977–78 academic year, courtesy of a grant from Notre Dame. Cathy had just graduated from Notre Dame and was settling in Chicago, Mary was a senior at Notre Dame, and Anne a sophomore in architecture. Anne spent half of that year in Rome, but she lived in the converted bordello Il Paradiso which Notre Dame had remodeled, and presumably exorcized, for a women's residence. So the family was reduced to Dave, Dan, and Beth. Our apartment that year was on the Via Aurelia, fourth floor, an apartment that had as many balconies as rooms. One of them overlooked the playing field of Notre Dame International, where the boys went to school. Beth was in Marymount, which was about as distant from the apartment as a school in Rome could possibly be. I drove her there in the morning and at first picked her up at night, but as the year progressed she became assured and independent and got herself home via city bus. I was now forty-eight, Connie would turn forty-six that year, and we would celebrate our silver anniversary.

The apartment was nicely furnished and the location was convenient, although the Via Aurelia was aroar with cars. But looking from our kitchen windows at the front of the building, one could see the fountain across the street. All day and night, it seemed, people would stop and fill huge jars with that water. Romans may not be wine snobs, but they are very particular about water and pledge allegiance to one source over another in impassioned tones. Beyond the fountain, over a crumbling wall, there were still open stretches, unbuilt. At night, prostitutes gathered on an island that separated the Aurelia from the ancient road that led across the Janiculum. In cold weather they broke boxes into kindling and built a fire to keep warm. From time to time a car would stop and negotiations begin, and, when successful, the woman would get into the car and it would head off to some secluded spot. In Rome, the whole spectrum of human behavior presents itself. The Aurelia leads on to the Anulare, the belt road around Rome, which in turn leads to the road to Fiumicino and the Leonardo da Vinci airport, a stretch that makes the Indianapolis Speedway seem tame.

Our old neighborhood has changed under the pressure of all this traffic. The eternal city may not change, but its temporal fringes are subject to the erosion of time. The local parish was Our Lady of Guadaloupe. On the Via Ugo Balzani we had attended St. Frances Cabrini Church, where the priests leaned over the dutch doors of their confessionals, absolving penitents with a wave of the hand. It was there, one Sunday, that the tiniest baby was baptized Massimo, something my sons never forgot. It was a name you could practice your Italian on.

When Beth and I would set out in the morning—we had another VW van—I would promise myself to be patient and rational, but before I had gone a block on the Via Aurelia I was shouting and yelling, totally maniacal. The Roman driver, while committing his outrages, is the picture of calmness. It is only when done in by another that the operetta begins. Sitting high in the VW, I had the impression of little Fiat bugs darting under my very wheels. Sometimes a car would simply take to the sidewalk to gain on others. What in God's name the hurry was, I do not know. Of course I do not mean to suggest that Romans are alone in being maddened by the feel of a steering wheel in their hands. In any case, my resolution to be patient and kind was never kept. I was very conscious of showing Beth a side of myself I would have liked to keep from my children, but of course children know us far better than we think. I suspect she enjoyed my road rage.

I divided my time between the Vatican Library and the American Academy, which was closer to our apartment. When I presented myself to pay my respects to the director, one John D'Arms, the son-in-law of Evelyn Waugh, I thought it was simply pro forma. He looked at me blankly and said I couldn't work there. Why not? Notre Dame had withdrawn its support for the American Academy. He was serious. In the Marine Corps we had a name for such punctiliousness. I told him I would write to Father Hesburgh and tell him the situation. I did. The provost, Father Burtchaell, had been cutting back on university financial commitments that seemed to him otiose, and the support for the American Academy was among the cuts. Father Hesburgh would never second-guess a subordinate. So I was in limbo. For all that, malgré d'Arms, I blithely used the library of the Academy as I worked on my Boethius and Aquinas book.

The Academy is a marvelous redoubt on the Janiculum where writers, musicians, and scholars pursue their various muses. As one walks the grounds, the sound of a piano comes drifting through the trees. The library had its charms; for me, it was the classical sources that made it useful. There was an elderly woman scholar who each day went through the same ritual. She would shuffle in, sighing and wheezing, get audibly settled at her table, and then bring forth a shoe box from which she extracted index cards. These she dealt out as if playing Solitaire. She arranged them carefully, she got her writing instruments in place, and when all was ready she would slump into herself and sleep. She slept most of the time she was there. When she awoke, the cards were gathered and replaced in the shoe box, and she struggled to her feet and shuffled off. I never asked who she was. She, too, soon became iconic for me. A warning. Scholarship is a lovely thing but it is dogged by the twin perils of pedantry and inconsequence. To know what others do not know, to be an expert in however restricted an area, is a powerful temptation. At mystery writers' conventions I have seen essentially the same skills applied to such questions as whose pseudonym was attached to stories published during a three- or four-year span of *Black Mask Magazine.* Does it really matter? Too much of what we do as scholars has little more intrinsic merit. In the humanities what is meant by research—a term now used in an incantatory way, as in "A

National Catholic Research University"—is by and large the uncovering of trivia. The world would not be a poorer place if 70 or 80 percent of "scholarly" publications had never been written. I speak as an offender.

It was a year of reunion with old friends, notably the Nortons. In Rome, Connie and Sally often got together. Several times we all were asked to the Abadia Celestina, which always made me feel I was entering the setting of an Agatha Christie mystery. The British School in Rome had published an account of the origins of the twelfth-century abbey whose remains were a feature of the Norton country place. There had been a re-burial of the bones found about the site, and the priest from the village that overlooks the abbey came for the purpose. Neither Guy nor Sally was Catholic, they would have described themselves more or less as Anglicans, which in Sally's case was manifested in her work for Oxfam. And of course they had lived in Rome for a long time. Wasn't it Cardinal Newman who said that it was not wise to get too close to the engine room of the bark of Peter? Still, the Nortons were moved by genuine *pietas* when they had those old bones reburied with ceremony.

At Christmas time we went on pilgrimage to the Holy Land, joining a Franciscan tour that set off from the Lateran. The security with which El Al protected its flights was unique at the time. Now of course it has become the rule. We were shuffled around the airport, put into a bus that seeemed to get lost but that suddenly darted toward a half-hidden plane, and were hastily shepherded aboard. We spent some days in Jerusalem, then went on to Bethlehem. We were there on Christmas Eve. The town was filled with youthful soldiers with grown-up guns. The greatest danger came when there was a stampede toward the Church of the Nativity for midnight Mass, but we survived. Connie and Beth were searched in a tent, the boys and I more publicly. Recently, in St. Paul, Minnesota, I saw a notice on the cathedral door announcing that it is illegal to bring fire arms into the church. One could take that as a text for meditation, one of those literal signs of the times that exfoliate in the imagination. A lesser spoor might be to wonder why the American Civil Liberties Union doesn't protest this breach of church-state separation. Perhaps they have. What was once rare and Middle Eastern is now commonplace and Midwestern.

In Nazareth, Connie came down with some bug and stayed in the hotel while the rest of us went off in Mercedes taxis to the Mount of Transfigu-

ration. What struck me about the sites we visited, the loci of the faith—
the places of the annunciation and the birth of Christ, Golgotha, the pillar at which Christ was scourged, the footprints in the rock said to have
been left when Christ ascended, the place of the visitation—was that
these sites were marked with plaques that had the relevant biblical texts
in various languages, with pride of place being given to the passages
from the Vulgate. I will not say this turned me into a Bible buff. My measure of that would-be Paul Claudel, and I am light-years distant from the
knowledge he gained over a long lifetime and wrote of so eloquently: a
large fraction of his *Oeuvres complètes* is dedicated to his biblical commentaries. But I did begin reading the New Testament in the Vulgate, I began to
buy bibles, I fiddled around with the Greek New Testament, and I bought
the Septuagint translated in Alexandria and even a Hebrew Bible, prom-
ising myself I would become halfway literate in Hebrew when I was old. I
still hope to keep that promise.

Our guide was a Basque priest named Pedro, who had lost a hand
in the Spanish Civil War. He was knowledgeable and fluent; the driver
of our bus was Michael. Whenever we stopped, children would run forward to sell us burnooses or carved camels, the price of which was uni-
formly "One dollah." Dave rode a camel. Two of his teachers from Notre
Dame International were with us, and they, too, unwisely boarded the
beast of the Magi. Mary from Lawton, Oklahoma, an old woman, won
our hearts by her way of saying, "I know, I KNOW," to whatever was said
to her. She was the widow of a military man and wanted to be sure we
knew all about Fort Lawton. Her sister, a Sister of the Holy Cross, was
with her, a study in contrasts.

■ Just before we set out for the Holy Land, early in December, I talked
with my mother for the last time on the telephone. Then came a call from
my brother telling me the end was near. I flew to Minneapolis, which was
undergoing the worse weather in half a century, with great piles of snow
and a temperature below zero. I took a cab to the hospital from the airport and was at my mother's bedside when she breathed her last. She died
on December 8, the feast of the Immaculate Conception. This is a holy day
of obligation, and my brothers and sisters, all nine of us, some spouses
too, went off to Holy Rosary, where my father had been an altar boy, to

hear Mass. Our unquestioned fulfillment of that obligation of Church law was more than a legalistic response. I felt my mother's influence on us all. At the funeral, Maurice, still unmarried, still as much a son as a man, sobbed aloud. Her absence was not cushioned for him by a wife. Shortly afterward he met Diane, as if to prove that Providence never runs out of surprises. Not just anyone could be a wife to Maurice, but that is probably true of us all. My dad needed support coming into and out of the church. His long love affair had reached its earthly end. My mother is buried in Resurrection cemetery, over the Mendota bridge from our neighborhood. My father joined her there nine years later, dying on December 19, 1986.

■   We traveled everywhere again, north, west, east, south—Dubrovnik and Yugoslavia were our entry to Greece this time. On our first sabbatical in Europe, we had only the oldest three children; on our second, all six; on our last, just the youngest three. My initial desire to go to Europe had a literary inspiration, but these sabbaticals made Europe a scholarly goal as well. In the past quarter of a century, I have gone off to Europe almost every year for three to four weeks on a writing vacation. Sometimes to France or Spain, but usually to Italy and of late, by preference, to Sicily. My practice is to settle into a hotel and write four stints a day. I have looked up from my computer onto the incredible blue of the Mediterranean from a window in Agrigento, the birthplace of Empedocles and Pirandello. Rapallo in the north has twice been the scene of such sojourns. When Connie and I traveled together our routine was quite different, of course. Most recently I spent three weeks in Ireland, where I had the most productive stay of all, working on these memoirs among other things. Of course Europe has changed since our first visit, and not for the better. It is not simply that lovely national currencies have given way to the euro. There is something post-Christian about the continent, England seems neo-pagan to me, and even holy Ireland is taking on the worst traits of modernity. Cardinal Schönborn has said that our cathedrals have become museums and our museums have become churches. That does not begin to capture the change that has occurred. For all that, I go back often and doubtless will continue to do so, most likely because my Europe was largely mythical from the beginning, a product of imagination and longing. That remains untouched by mere reality.

In 1999–2000, I gave the Gifford Lectures at the University of Glasgow, where Alexander Broadie, with an unnerving physical resemblance to Wittgenstein, was a genial host, constant companion, and the default first questioner at each of my ten lectures. Broadie once told me that there are two kinds of Jew in Scotland, Protestant Jews and Catholic Jews. "I am a Catholic Jew." Connie and Sally Norton, who had been touring Scotland, were there for my inaugural lecture and the elegant reception and dinner that followed.

In the spring of 2003, I gave the Joseph lectures at the Gregorianum in Rome, living in a cottage on the grounds of the Irish College, near St. John Lateran. I was there for months but took a quick trip to Houston to deliver the commencement address at the University of St. Thomas and receive an honorary degree, my eighth. My son Danny had resigned from the faculty there, and I was glad of the opportunity to show that there were no hard feelings. When I returned to Rome, I was at work in my cottage on *Praeambula Fidei*, the sequel to my Gifford lectures, when a face appeared in the open window and asked me about my trip to Texas. I answered, the conversation went on, and then I said, "Good Lord, you're Bob Wilken!" And so he was. He was in the next cottage, and we renewed our acquaintance. He had taught at Notre Dame before going on to the University of Virginia.

A feature of that stay was the Dante group I was asked to join. Two young Jesuits, Father Mankowski and Father Flannery, my host at the "Greg," would meet in Flannery's office each Sunday evening, recite vespers, go to the dining room for supper, return, say compline, and then open a bottle of red wine and our copies of the *Paradiso*. We took turns translating. Afterward, I would walk home past the Colosseum. One night I was approached by a disheveled young man who asked me for directions. After he left me, two men appeared, claiming to be cops, and wanted to know if I had bought drugs from the first man. In the course of their accusations, I got out my wallet to show my identification. One of them took it and studied it, the other kept me occupied with accusations. When they released me, I felt I had been given a reprieve by the governor. It was half a mile before doubt set in. I checked my wallet. All but a few bills were gone. To be robbed in Rome has ruined many a stay, but I was more embarrassed by my simplicity than angered by my loss. It was weeks before I told Mankowski and Flannery what had happened.

Several times a year I go to Rome for meetings, usually of the Pontifical Academy of St. Thomas Aquinas, sometimes staying in the Vatican in the Domus Sanctae Marthae, which housed the cardinals during the conclave that elected Joseph Ratzinger as Benedict XVI. As often as not, when I am in Rome, I will go by the apartments where we spent sabbatical years and let the sweet sad memories come. It is pleasant to recall my children when they were young, in the morning of their lives, and when Connie and I were all in all to them. Now they are middle-aged and I am old, but those addresses which were ours for a year can for a moment erase the intervening years and I feel merely forty again.

AUTHOR

IT IS THE RARE READER OF FICTION WHO DOES NOT AT SOME TIME OR other consider becoming a writer himself. As a velleity it comes and goes over the years for many, and some carry it about forever as an unredeemed promissory note to themselves. In their heart of hearts, they regard themselves as writers. Unfortunately, they never write anything. When my first novel appeared I got a note from a senior colleague to the effect that it was sly of me not only to think of writing a novel but actually to do it. The capacity, apparently, like depravity for Calvin, was taken to be universal. How often our congratulations are self-referential, implicit boomerangs.

Of course everyone can write; everyone knows English. This is doubtless the source of the conviction that one is already a writer without having published—one has always written. Letters anyway, and what is fiction but a variation on the sentences and paragraphs any literate person can construct? I do not mock this, because it was my own case for so long. In my early teens I saw myself as a writer, I became fascinated with biographies of authors, I idolized the upper classmen who produced the poems and stories and articles for the school magazine. Eventually, I myself would be an upperclassman who wrote for and edited that magazine. Throughout my non-hazardous hitch in the Marine Corps I thought of myself as prepping for the commencement of my writing career when I would once again be a civilian. My return to the seminary did not really alter this. In my seminary years of philosophy I wrote a verse play and I even began a novel. With my veteran's allowance I bought a box full of past numbers of the *Partisan Review.* In poring over them I came upon J. F. Powers's "St. Paul Home of the Saints."

Powers was a layman, but he was a legend among priests in St. Paul. His *Prince of Darkness and Other Stories* showed such an uncanny knowledge of the trivia of local clerical life that it was presumed he had some priestly informant who fed him gossip for his stories. His portrait of Archbishop John Gregory Murray in the title story of that collection seemed drawn from life. Of course it is libelous to suggest that Powers's importance lies in the accuracy of his settings. In any case, like all fictional settings, they were created rather than borrowed. The importance of Powers lay in the fact that he had put together priests and fiction. I mean, naturally, his importance for me. What the significance was for me that this layman wrote about priests I could not then guess, but it was as if some barrier had been removed. There was also a novel written by a St. Paul priest, Keeler, *The Burden Light,* which told of a newly ordained young man's first clerical assignment. If Powers's stories were etched in India ink, this little novel was in pastels.

Many years later, when I was director of the Wethersfield Foundation, I contrived an award for Powers in the hope of luring him to New York. After much coaxing, he agreed to come if a former dean could accompany him. Powers was anything but a platform performer, and I am afraid that not many in the audience knew his work. For all that, his talk is included in the book that resulted from the conference. One of the things that had tipped the balance in favor of his coming was the prospect of hearing jazz. We stood one night on a corner, waiting for the light to change, and Powers looked toward Central Park. Did I know Garrison Keillor? I know who he is. He lives up there. Then Powers squinted at me. "Imagine how much money you would have to earn to afford to live there." Perhaps this was an oblique statement of his creed as a writer. He lived simply, ending in an apartment on the campus of St. John's University after his wife died. I doubt that Powers's lifetime earnings could have paid a year's rent on a Central Park apartment. He had lived in such a way that he could write at his own pace, with no temptation to speed up the production line to meet unnecessary expenses. For all that, there was a wistful look on his face when he looked toward Garrison Keillor's presumably sumptuous digs.

When I left the seminary for the second time, certain now that the priesthood was not my vocation, I was not the same man who entered. I had begun the study of philosophy. I began graduate studies in philosophy. Philosophical prose is for the most part as distant from the imaginative use of language as one can get. Dullness is all. Dullness and clarity, that is. (Beware of a philosopher when he boasts of being clear and distinct.) At the age of twenty-two, any literary ambitions of mine were going to have to be compatible with my academic involvement. Among the books I bought in the summer before graduate school were W. H. Auden's *Collected Poetry* and his more recent *Nones*. They are still on my shelves. Writing in the fullest sense meant poetry, and everything else declined from that like cases of a noun. And so, employed in the bottle house of the Grain Belt beer company, working nights, I would wake in the attic bedroom of my grandmother's house—my family were in Wisconsin for the summer—and try to write poetry. When graduate school began and I spent a couple of months working nights on a punch press, I found myself surrounded by people who considered themselves artists. One of them confided to me that his ambition was to write pornographic novels. He mentioned an author whose descriptions of mating were so metaphorically sedate that they would have sailed over innocent heads and failed to stuff other heads with the explicit reenactments they were after. So he had a mission. If you're going to write a dirty book, make it dirty. I have often thought of that fellow. What if he tried and failed? Pornography aims below the belt and only mimics fiction. A good pornographic novel may be an oxymoron, and I don't mean morally good. If you try to write something worthwhile, and succeed at least in part, yet fail to find a publisher, the defeat is not total. You still have what you wrote. But what would you do with a rejected pornographic manuscript?

At the University of Minnesota and at Laval, at first single and then married, I continued to write. I sent a Christmas poem to fellow students and to some of the faculty, and Charles De Koninck was impressed all out of proportion to the value of the poems I showed him. (Later I would discover that he had attempted to write a novel.) During the months that I was writing my dissertation I was also at work on a novel. Since I never throw anything away, I cannot rewrite such things in memory and lament the loss of something precious. It is penitential for me to even page through those early efforts. There was another novel written in Omaha, and yet another when we moved to South Bend in August 1955. I sat at the dining room table in my bathing trunks because of the ungodly heat and wrote a novel. Over the years I would occasionally write a short story and mail it in, my preferred target being *The New Yorker*. It would come back, in Thurber's phrase, like a serve in tennis. What I remember about those years was how episodic my efforts were. After I sent off a story, I would wait as if for news of the Nobel Prize. Rejection was cushioned by no work in progress. I was not serious.

On January 16, 1964, I decided to get serious. We had moved into the house on Portage Avenue and were overextended. Getting through the month was depressingly reminiscent of days we thought we had left behind forever. I took on teaching a couple courses at IUSB (the branch of Indiana University in South Bend), adding those to my daily chores at Notre Dame, but this was peanuts. I remembered the copy of *Writer's Digest* I had bought in the Los Angeles train station in 1946. I decided that I would write for commercial markets, not just sporadically, but determinedly, every day, and keep at it for a year, after which if I had not sold anything I would admit to myself that I was not really a writer.

And so it began. In the basement was a workbench, unlikely to serve its original purpose for me. It became my desk. It was L-shaped. I plunked my typewriter on the short leg of the L and, standing, began. Every night, after we had put the kids to bed and spent some time together, I would go downstairs and write from ten until about two in the morning. The markets I was chiefly interested in were *Redbook, Ladies Home Journal, Good Housekeeping*. Their initial price for a story was a thousand dollars. I sent stories out, but I was always ready with others when they came back. There was never a time when I wasn't awaiting editorial word on one or more stories. This gave room for hope. In April I began to get messages on the rejection slips and then a letter from an editor at *Redbook*, Sandra Earl, telling me "close but no cigar," and urging me to keep trying.

Those early times at my converted workbench were, I came to see, my apprenticeship. For someone who aspired to write fiction I was almost totally ignorant of how a story is made. The slick magazines operated on the Edgar Allan Poe principle that a story aims at a single effect. No sideshows, nothing that does not contribute to the point of the story. I would sometimes be asked what paragraph three on page seven was meant to do, would read it, find it lovely writing, of course, but also find it effectively idle in the story. Out it went. I was learning that one writes for a reader. Writing is too often described as self-expression. But writing is the art of making a story that will engage and hold and satisfy the interest of the reader. Lint from one's navel seldom has this effect. I typed a slogan and pinned it over my typewriter. Nobody Owes You A Reading.

What I thought were stories piled up on the workbench. Most went into the mail. With time I began to see why they were rejected. They weren't stories. And what is a story? An attractive or at least intriguing character faces a crucial choice. The story is the account of his making it, solving his problem, resolving a dilemma. His efforts worsen rather than ease his situation. Eventually he arrives at the dark moment when all seems lost. Then, by his own efforts, plausibly but surprisingly, he succeeds. Story's over. A variation on this is the villain whose pursuit of his evil goal triumphs over one obstacle after another until, just as ultimate success seems assured, surprisingly but plausibly, he goes down in flames.

Is this formula fiction? Well, you can find this account of imaginative portrayals of human agents in Aristotle's *Poetics.* The structure I have just sketched is of course the plot, what gives a narrative a beginning, a middle, and an end, in Aristotle's pithy phrase. Or, in Peter De Vries's version, a beginning, a muddle, and an end. Plot is not everything, but it is the soul of the story. E. M. Forster, in *Aspects of the Novel,* adopting his most precious style, laments that the novelist must provide a plot for the unwashed reader. If only one could write for one's friends at Cambridge, plot could be dispensed with and . . . and what? Essays? Dialogue? Mood settings? Like most writers, Forster ignored his own advice. If he hadn't, you would never have heard of him.

I sold my first story before the year was out to *Redbook,* a story called "The First Farewell." It was based on Cathy and Mary's going to school in Louvain. Many years later, a young woman who did her doctorate with me, Pat Guinan, handset this story in type and produced a wonderful Christmas presentation volume on home-made paper, printing and binding four copies for me. I dedicated it, as I would so many of my books, to Connie. The themes of the stories I wrote for the magazines were domestic—the kids going to camp, recitals, trouble at school. All I had to do was look around my house and see the germs of stories. It was Connie who suggested the basis for "The First Farewell."

I began publishing under a pseudonym, Ernan Mackey, an anagram on my family name. Why? To keep my fiction separate from my academic career. At the beginning I felt more divided than I did later between two non-overlapping kinds of writing. I went to New York and met the editors with whom I had been corresponding. Sandy Earl took me around the *Redbook* offices and showed me the reports the fiction department prepared and explained the politicking involved in getting a story accepted. She, I now realized, was my champion there. I watched the receptionist, who served as the first reader of unsolicited manuscripts, draw pages from a manila envelope, read a few lines, let the pages drop back and set it aside for rejection. She took these from what was called the slush pile. It was from that pile that I myself had been plucked. How easily it might not have happened. As often as not, that woman did not have to read more than a few lines to tell whether it was a story or not, and if it was, whether it would be of interest to *Redbook*'s readers. Once taken up by an editor, one sent things directly to her. But it was unnerving to see how narrow the gateway was. All that has changed long since. Few magazines will even open unsolicited manuscripts; the open sesame now is through an agent.

I don't think it's harder to get published now, only different. When I began it was common to complain about the number of magazines that had folded. Why, in the good old days. . . . All true, no doubt, but so what? There were still plenty of magazines around. As I have come to realize, learning how to sell stories to those magazines forced me to learn the craft of writing. When I did, I managed to redeem most of those non-stories that had piled up beside my typewriter and had been the cause of lots of wasted postage. Now I could read them with a craftsman's eye and as often as not find the story I had ruined and bring it out of the misshaped marble and redeem it. I was lucky, of course. Every published writer is the beneficiary of luck. But the luck has to have something to work with. Among my good fortune was the fact that editors began to treat me as if they were my aunts. They were all women, of course. The editor in chief might be male, but the work of the magazines was done by women. There were no men in the fiction departments. On one of my visits to New York, three or four editors from different magazines sat me down in the Algonquin, plied me with manhattans, and discussed my career. It was now three years since my big resolution. I was selling stories regularly. One year I sold more stories to *Redbook* than anyone else ever had, using several pen names. It was the consensus of the group that I was ready for more. I needed an agent. They supplied me with a short list of agents they had agreed on, and I went around to their offices and in effect interviewed them. Liz Christman, who would end up on the faculty at Notre Dame and become a dear friend, worked with Harold Ober at the time and remembered my visit to Ober's agency. It was Henry Volkening, however, who became my first agent.

Henry's office was in the French Building on Park Avenue. He had the diffidence of a drinker, and indeed when he took me to the Century Club for lunch, we largely drank it, or at least Henry did, ringing the bell on the table for another martini and unnecessarily telling me not to try to keep up with him. His schedule seemed to be to take the bus to his office very early and work all morning and then, lunch. . . . Drink may be the one vice that has attendant virtues. Humbled by the habit, one seems to become more tolerant of others, kinder, magnanimous. Whatever the truth of that, Henry was a gentle man. Listening to him sum up his own career made me realize that he was my connection with the mythical past. He had begun at Scribner's, where no less an editor than Maxwell Perkins had told him that there was more need for good agents than for another editor. So with Diarmid Russell, the son of the Irish writer who signed himself AE, he founded an agency.

I was the last client Henry took on. He assured me without altering his tone that I would be a success as a writer. I felt knighted by the words. He had visited Notre Dame and knew my colleague Dick Sullivan—Dick was one of his clients—but apart from that we had little in common. I was young, he was in his sixties, he represented writers who were household names and as their agent took care of all the business details, of course, but like Russell, it was writing that remained Henry's passion. Eudora Welty has written a book about her long association with the agency, and in it there are photographs of the partners in their youth. The Henry I came to know had a valedictory air. He typed his own letters, and of course typing in those days was a physical act. From the outset, he let me know he didn't like my use of a pseudonym: "It's hard enough to make one name famous, let alone two." He said things like that. He was not thinking of my magazine stories. Something had happened.

It was the spring of 1965. Cornelio Fabro was a visiting professor at Notre Dame, with rooms in the infirmary, and he showed me a piece he had published in Italy called "Il Tomismo di domani"—The Thomism of Tomorrow. Vatican II was winding down, and there was a lot of talk about the role of philosophy and of Thomas Aquinas in the post-conciliar church. I suggested to the editors of *America* that I translate Fabro's article for them. Well, they liked the topic but it was too long. Why didn't I write my own article, with a more American cast to it? I did. It was "Thomism in an Age of Renewal." Jack Bernard, an editor at Doubleday, saw it and wrote to ask if I would like to develop it into a book. I did. Later, at lunch in New York with Jack, I listened to him say nice things about the manuscript I had turned in. He liked the way I wrote. I told him that I also wrote fiction. "Really? Have you ever thought of writing a novel?" If I hadn't, I would have thought of it then and there. There was a story I had written under the influence of J. P. Donleavy called "Jolly Rogerson." I had sent it to the *Paris Review* and there it sat, unrejected, untaken. That story came into my mind and suddenly seemed part of something larger. "Yes," I said. "I am thinking of writing a novel." "When you finish it, let me see it."

Here, at a crucial point in my fiction-writing career, my academic work had proved to give me an entrée I might otherwise never have had. I was a Doubleday author, my editor was asking about my next book. It all seemed quite natural, but how easily it might not have happened. Talking with other writers over the years I have learned that just about everyone's career involves this moment of happenstance without which the future would have been very different. Luck is a necessary but not sufficient condition of success. Far more important is the habit of going down to one's workbench, day after day, and doing one's pages. My resolution had made me a disciplined writer, which is the only kind I can admire. Perhaps it is the only kind there is. Trollope, and his mother Fanny before him, are legendary for their early morning writing, every day, done before other tasks made their claim. Those with a romantic conception of how stories and novels get written profess shock at the matter-of-fact way Trollope described his craft, likening it to making shoes. Writing classes, I have found, attract romantics. Talk of the craft, of the technique required to catch and hold the reader's attention, seem like selling out. Shouldn't the writer, quill pen in hand, soulful eyes lifted, attend to the Muse? Trollope's autobiography is often an effective antidote to this. Trollope also knew to a penny the amount of money he had made as a writer, but then so did F. Scott Fitzgerald. Professional writers do not write for money as the main purpose of what they do, but it is of course one aim and an important one. To be paid for what you have written is an unequivocal sign that it is valued.

This was my situation as I spoke with Henry Volkening. No doubt it was pleasant to take on a client who already had a track record with magazines, but here I was with a contract for a novel as well. After that lunch with Jack the previous spring I had gone home, got out "Jolly Rogerson" the story, and expanded it into what would prove to be my first published novel. Henry seemed less than enthusiastic about Doubleday and arranged for me to meet Robert Giroux at Farrar Straus. Henry was not of course suggesting that I try to get out of an agreement; he was looking ahead.

When I set out to write *Jolly Rogerson* I was in a very different situation than I had been when I wrote those dubious novels of yore. Writing short stories had forced me to learn the basics of technique, things that were applicable to longer as well as shorter efforts. One effect of the short story writing was that I conceived and wrote the novel in segments which were about the length of a magazine story, then more or less 3,500 to 4,000 words. The only guide I had as I set out, apart from the short story that went almost unchanged into the second part of the novel, was a list of three words: Failure, Success, Beyond. I was to write two more novels featuring Matthew Rogerson: *Rogerson at Bay* and *The Search Committee*. They are the funniest books I have ever published. I myself am now distant enough from them that I can read them and roll on the floor while doing so. In the privacy of my own mind, I tell myself that I was pretty good in those days. Rogerson is forty-four, which seemed an advanced age to me as I wrote the first novel. He is a flop in every department of his life—in his marriage, as a father, as a teacher. The first part establishes this and ends with Rogerson vowing to accept his fate and to elevate his failure to epic proportions. And of course in the second part these efforts to fail are shown to fail, and Rogerson is suddenly covered with all the emblems of success. The third part takes him to the point of rejecting both the concepts of success and those of failure, these terms being conferred whimsically by others and not signs of personal achievements. That makes it sound pretty cerebral, and I could not have written such a description at the outset of writing the novel. But it did develop with ease and naturalness. Those were good hours spent standing at my typewriter, from time to time looking up at Nobody Owes You A Reading and that list: Failure, Success, Beyond. The basement windows are open, it is summer, I can hear my children playing in the yard. Connie is out there too, gardening. It was the best of times.

I finished the novel and sent it in and it was accepted. Not even God can change the past. But the past could have been utterly different. I could have run into problems trying to write a novel and settled for writing short stories. I could have sent it in and had it rejected. At every point of my writing efforts there has been that sort of either/or. Either the magazines would continue to be interested in my stories or they would not, for example. I certainly had not reached the point where acceptance was assured simply because I had already sold so many stories. Each one had to stand by itself. So too with novels. It was because I was so conscious of the chanciness of what I was doing that I did not burden Connie with a lot of details. What had she thought when I said I would make extra money by writing fiction? She knew that I had been writing fiction since we met, writing in a desultory way, but nonetheless writing. She knew of the novels, not least of them *If Salt Lose Its Savor,* a book as bad as its title that I had written the first summer in South Bend, and *The Middle of Next Week,* the mystery novel I had written on Rexford Drive. These, like the stories that had gone off over the years, had led to nothing. Why should it be any different now? Well, I was serious now. And Connie would have seen that seriousness because of the schedule I had devised. But we never sat around and discussed my future as a writer. I wanted her in on the landings, but not the crashes. We must have talked a bit about what I was up to down there. It was Connie who suggested the idea of the kids starting school in Louvain as a story, and it was the first one I sold. But by and large, I did not trouble her with the hopes and dreams and dashed expectations of my writing. My academic career provided more than enough drama and involved a public stage. When good things happened they thus had some element of surprise in them, and Connie enjoyed them more than she would have if, like me, literary success had been something I had awaited with fear and trembling that it might not happen. And of course there was the money. She always took care of that.

Jolly Rogerson got good reviews, and everyone seemed pleased, not that it sold a lot of copies. Among the things it meant was that my writing could now rejoin its original aspiration. When I first started mooning about it—not in the sense of the Rodney Dangerfield joke about being arrested for mooning when he looked out the window—writing had little to do with agents and sales and reviews; it was an ethereal transaction between the writer and God. It was serious. Writing stories on domestic and romantic themes for the women's magazines had got us out of debt and more, but writing for such magazines had not been among the dreams of my youth. For three years I had happily written story after story for them, and whatever the restraints of the magazines—they imagined their typical reader to be a young wife of about thirty years old with a couple of kids—I seldom found them colliding with what I was writing. Sometimes this did happen. For example, I wrote a story called "I Don't Want To Be Like You," in which a father comes to campus to talk sense into his son who is living with a girl. The father has brought his secretary along. The son discovers this, all paternal authority is gone, and the son utters the title. Well, *Redbook* liked it, but I had told it from the viewpoint of the father. Too old. It was a small matter to rewrite the story from the viewpoint of the son, and that is how it appeared. This taught me how to recycle story ideas. The average number of characters in a short story is three or four. The story is told from the viewpoint of one of them. What would it look like told from another viewpoint? Episodes change, and the result both is and is not the same story.

Redbook had an August issue that contained twice as much fiction as usual. The usual was three short stories, one short short, and one novel. My novella *A Season of Endings,* heavily influenced by Fitzgerald's *Winter Dreams,* appeared in an August issue. But I became very adept at the short short, a thousand-word story. I have looked again at the stories I wrote for the magazines and did not wince. Some of them could have appeared anywhere. There is none I would not acknowledge. I say that because many of them appeared under a pen name. Of course, as the history of the short story "Jolly Rogerson" indicates, I was not restricting myself to the slicks. I continued to send things to such magazines as *Paris Review,* the *New Yorker,* and so on. But Jack Bernard's suggestion provided the opportunity to turn the skills I had acquired to more ambitious fictional ends.

Second novels are notoriously fateful. Can one repeat a successful performance? I started to write *A Narrow Time* in an A-frame cottage on Lake Michigan where we were vacationing with the kids. I was out to dazzle and amaze. The novel would be experimental; there would be parts that would be written as scenes in a play—shades of *This Side of Paradise*—it would be impressive. In short, I was showing off, drawing attention to myself. Anne Freedgood had succeeded Jack Bernard as my editor at Doubleday. She gently steered me away from all the razzle-dazzle. All it took was an oblique question or two about what I showed her; I looked at it again and saw how sophomoric it was. I started over, remembered what I had learned, and wrote the novel. It deals with the effect on a young couple of losing a child. It was risky for me to take on such a theme, and perhaps that was why I had tried to obscure it with fireworks. It is a sad and funny story, better, I think, than *Jolly Rogerson.* In the summer of 1969 we were preparing to go to Rome for the year and *A Narrow Time* would be published in October. So prepublication copies were going around to reviewers. I got a call from *Time.* They wanted to send a reporter and photographer from their Chicago office to Notre Dame to interview me about my new novel.

The reporter came and we walked around the campus, me being photographed as we did, talking about my new novel which the reporter hadn't read. So we talked about my aims as a writer and the apparent oddity that I also taught philosophy, about my wife and kids, about Notre Dame, everything under the sun. He was very good. When he left he was enthusiastic about the interview. When we were marooned in Halifax I began to check out issues of *Time* to find the article that was going to catapult me into fame. It wasn't there. Ah, but the Canadian edition of *Time* is not identical to the United States edition. Perhaps it had already appeared and I didn't know it. Well, it never did appear. That sort of thing happens. I was disappointed, but I have come to think it was all for the best. What was in store for me was a long career, not at all flashy, the performance of a long-distance runner. Maybe an article in *Time* would have made me a sprinter and I would have burned out long ago.

In the fall of 1969, in Rome, I drafted what would become *The Priest,* some thirteen hundred pages of manuscript. The agent I had hooked up with after Henry Volkening died I had yet to meet. It was at her office that my son Dave and I dropped off some stories for her to sell. She was not in. I was her client for a little more than a year. She nearly put me out of business. I had been selling stories regularly, and she could not sell one. Worse, I sent her what I was working on, and she treated it as a finished product and showed it to Anne Freedgood. When I had told Anne what the next novel would be about, she said she thought it would be my breakthrough novel. As it happened, she was right, but it took a few years to find that out. Anne judged that what she was shown was in need of work, as indeed it was. My agent, who shall be nameless, wanted to try the manuscript elsewhere. I was in Rome, she was in New York, she would write me in care of American Express. I was not in direct contact with Anne Freedgood. Like an ass, I told the agent to try to place it elsewhere. Had I forgotten that the novel was sprawling, inchoate, in need of work? The agent spoke of going down her list with the manuscript, anticipating rejections. We got them, one after another. Finally, I told her to stop. Just hold off until I got home. When I got home I dropped her. In the course of one year, from the heady experience of the *Time* interview, my name was mud at the magazines and at Doubleday. I had left the country with a publisher; I returned a writer whose third novel seemed to have bombed.

This was a tough time. Taking a family to Europe, having six kids in private schools, travel, all the rest, costs a lot. Who cared? We depleted our savings to make the year memorable, and it was. Home again, I realized how dependent we had become on my earnings as a writer. My predicament was worse than I had let on to Connie. I could very well have been finished. I got back on my old schedule, I sold a story or two, but there on the workbench was that big pile of pages of my third novel that represented failure. I would have liked to think only of those wonderful Roman mornings when I had sat at the typewriter, doing my stint, so Connie and I could hit the town for lunch. I tried to revive the novel. Henry Regnery had been the original publisher of the five-volume history of philosophy that Bob Caponigri and I wrote. I had got to know him to some extent; he was an extraordinary man, a publisher who published only books on which he was proud to have his name. What did he think of the novel I was working on? He was kind, but Regnery did not publish novels, as I knew; I had presented the possibility as an interesting departure.

What was the novel about? It was set in 1968 and the central character was a young priest, Frank Ascue, just returned from Rome to begin teaching moral theology at the Fort Elbow, Ohio, seminary. The question I had put myself was: what is it like to be a young priest today when the Church seems to be reeling in post-conciliar factionalism? I had envisaged a short, focused book, but the more I thought of it the more various and complicated the background seemed. I expanded my cast, I multiplied subplots, I provided a pretty good portrait of what the Church looked like in the wake of Vatican II. I had liked it when I wrote it. I still liked it. I began to revise and tighten. And then I did what turned everything around.

I never throw things away, so I still had a letter that Theron Raines sent me after *Jolly Rogerson* came out, in which he wondered if I had an agent. I kept the letter. Now, three years later, I answered it as if I had just received it and sent a sample of what I was working on. He telephoned. This was 1971. All my dealings to this point had been by letter or face to face. That phone call was a turning point. Theron was enthused about what I had sent him. He spoke matter-of-factly of its being a major novel. After the doldrums I had been in, this was more than welcome news. We became agent and client, and with Theron's encouragement and his ability to convey enthusiasm in a voice that suggested he was dropping off to sleep, I rewrote my novel and we called it *The Priest*. While I was working on it I called it *Where No Storms Come,* from the Hopkins poem that prefaces the story, but that was too poetic. Theron placed it with Harper & Row, and my editor became Buz Wyeth. In the final stages of the novel, Wyeth asked me to his place up on the Hudson River, where he had beehives and a nice old house filled with photographs of family and friends. He was a vice president at Harper & Row, and he was convinced that big things lay ahead.

Well, they did. *The Priest* is the only bestseller I have had. In hardback, bookclub editions, and paperback, it sold a million copies and more. In those days paperback deals were big deals, and I got a bundle for the reprint rights. Within a couple of years of our return from Rome and a writing career that seemed over, I was suddenly at the top of the heap. Harper sent me around to sign books. On several jaunts I was linked with the actor Tom Tryon, who wore a white suit and had written an odd novel for Harper. He had also played the cardinal in the movie made from Henry Morton Robinson's novel of that title, but I thought of him as Mac in *In Harm's Way*. I did a lot better on the tour circuit when I wasn't eclipsed by a movie actor.

To have a novel do that well is a mixed blessing, as I came to see. Everyone assumes that from now on you will be writing books that will be received at least as well, preferably better. Your agent asks for and gets a hefty advance. No one really knows why some books sell and others do not. If they did, all books would sell well. *The Priest* was the story I set out to tell, and its success was a bonus. Even if there were some way in which one could repeat, I would not have been interested. I wanted to write what

I wanted to write and let the chips fall where they might. What does the Church look like to an old priest? This question complemented that asked in *The Priest.* And so I wrote *Gate of Heaven,* which is set in a retirement home for priests who see everything they gave their lives to crumbling around them. When I decided on a wide canvas for *The Priest,* I naturally made use of the technique of multiple viewpoint; this enabled me to let all the different views and opinions be represented by a character who held them. I had also used multiple viewpoint in *Gate of Heaven.* It was one of my better novels, if I do say so myself, but even as I wrote I doubted that it would have the demotic appeal of *The Priest.* One thing that had become clear to me was that Catholic things which were ordinary and everyday for me had an exotic appeal to someone like Theron Raines. The only direct advice he gave me was to expand the final ruminations of Frank Ascue. And then expand them more. He began to talk of Dostoevsky.

The new novel was not only churchy, it was clerical, and there was scarcely a character in it less that seventy years old. It was published in 1975. It was not a bestseller. I detected a note of disappointment. I have sometimes wondered how things would have gone if, instead of writing *Gate of Heaven* next, I had written the sequel to *Jolly Rogerson* that followed it, *Rogerson at Bay.* Buz Wyeth solicited some very impressive puffs for the latter book. It was called the funniest novel in years. It is funny. I recently reread it. I laughed aloud. I am not that easy to please.

■ Some writers write a lot, others write little, and this has nothing to do with whether they write well or badly. One man's haste is another's jogging, and vice versa. Over the years I have collected literary biography, a practice that began more or less accidentally when I bought a remaindered copy of Mark Schorer's life of Sinclair Lewis, which should have put me off the genre. Seldom has a biographer taken a more condescending attitude toward his subject or measured him by standards wholly irrelevant to what he set out to do. That Lewis did not write for *The New Masses* is taken to be evidence that he was not serious. For all that, Lewis triumphed over his biographer. In reading lives of writers, I was particularly on the *qui vive* for information about the nuts and bolts of the writing life, its infrastructure, so to speak. How long did it take Lewis to write one of his novels, how much did he write each day? Where? When? With what? Trivia, perhaps, but it is what makes another writer vivid to me. It always amazes me how little this sort of thing interests most biographers. With someone like Trollope such facts are unavoidable; he himself put them in the center of his own account of his writing. I should add that Lewis is no particular favorite of mine. The fact that he was a fellow Minnesotan was in his favor, of course, but much of his outlook is unsympathetic to me. In stark contrast to Schorer's life is Victoria Glendenning's life of Trollope. She is a late-twentieth-century feminist, much of what Trollope took for granted about the relation between the sexes is unsympathetic to her, and yet she has written what I regard as the best life of the novelist, and there have been several very good ones.

All this is to make the point that I write a lot. The way I started writing seriously, the urgency of succeeding, doggedly and daily sticking with it, led to a pile of manuscripts. I wrote something like sixty stories the first year on the job, and, as I have said, most of them eventually found their way into print. The transition to novels suggested slowing down. To publish a novel a year would be to court the condescension long shown toward Joyce Carol Oates, who is a prolific writer. It seemed axiomatic to many reviewers that no one who wrote that much could do it well. And even when they found no signs of haste or sloppiness it was de rigueur to mention how much she published. So what? But from a marketing point of view, publishers seemed to expect that every two or three years they would receive a new manuscript. For me this was as unattractive as birth control. I suggested to Theron that it might be fun to add a pseudonym or two and write more. Perhaps these ruminations lay behind a suggestion he made in the summer of 1976.

He telephoned, and there was what passed for excitement in his voice. "I have a great idea." He had been reading Harry Kemelman's mystery series, which featured a rabbi. I had written two novels featuring priests. Why didn't I start a series using a priest detective? My reaction was mixed. The suggestion that I write mystery novels seemed a retrogression. I had graduated from the slick magazines, or at least to exclusive appearances there. I was a novelist. I was a writer. Mysteries? Of course I also thought of Chesterton's Father Brown stories and was not wild about the thought of inviting comparison with those, even though the Father Brown stories are all short stories. Once at Nazareth Hall I had faked illness and retired to the infirmary with *The Father Brown Omnibus* and read them all. There was also the sneaking suspicion that I couldn't write a mystery.

I had tried one, back in my dilettante days, but that didn't count. What I assumed was that in order to write a mystery, one would have to work the thing out beforehand. Sinclair Lewis had written thirty-page single-spaced treatments of novels before he began them. These were effectively the basic plot, which he then went on to dramatize. I tried that once. When I was done I had lost interest in the idea. From the beginning my practice had been to think through the story as I did the first draft. I would begin with the vaguest notion of what I would write and make it specific as I went. I had carried this over to novels. Could you write a mystery that way?

Two things decided me to respond to Theron's suggestion. I made a study of Rex Stout's Nero Wolfe mysteries, reading them now as a writer. Archie Goodwin is the narrator and lives with Wolfe in an old brownstone in Manhattan. There is a cook and of course a gardener, who works on the orchids in the rooftop conservatory. Wolfe is lazy and Archie has to spur him to take a client, usually by pointing out that the cost of running the establishment is outrunning income. Okay. A knock on the door. Perhaps a man from the Midwest, whose daughter came to New York and seems to have disappeared. Reluctantly Wolfe takes the case, meaning that Archie gets to work on it. The girl's body shows up in the morgue. The next phase consists of Archie, along with some helpers, getting to know maybe nine or ten people connected with the missing girl. It dawned on me that these were in effect the suspects. The next phase was to eliminate the suspects one by one, sometimes by having them killed. The ideal is to have Archie and the police, namely Inspector Cramer, following false scents and confessing failure. Then comes the finale. A number of the suspects are invited to Wolfe's study, Cramer is there, and so of course is Archie. The great man reviews what has been learned and then, surprisingly, plausibly, explains how the girl died. One of the guests leaps to his feet. Cramer subdues him. Case closed.

What occurred to me as I saw this pattern disclose itself in title after title was that Stout did not have to know at the outset who did it. He could let that work itself out as he wrote. Many more ideas come in the course of writing than could ever come beforehand. That was one obstacle out of the way. The second was a lesser one, but not to me. I had discovered that multiple viewpoint was my natural way of presenting a story. Could a mystery be told in this way? Agatha Christie, I discovered, had done it. By this time, I was very curious to see if I could bring it off.

In the summer of 1976, I gave some preliminary thought to the characters who would recur if a series developed. I began to have a notion of what Father Dowling was like. As a priest, he might seem to be observing everything from a lofty point of view, so I made him a recovered alcoholic, chastened by what he had been through and a better man and priest because of it. Phil Keegan, a widower who had washed out of the seminary because he couldn't master Latin, is a detective of police in Fox River, my imaginary Illinois town in the orbit of Chicago. And I thought of Marie Murkin, the housekeeper, inspired by one in a J. F. Powers story. I then drafted two novels with these characters, to see if I could do it, and to see if Theron thought I could. I sent them to him. He placed them with Vanguard. I was a mystery writer.

Beginning with *Her Death of Cold*, I have now published twenty-four Father Dowling mysteries. I have also published a great many other mysteries until now I am regarded, if regarded at all, as a mystery writer. From time to time I write a novel in the ordinary sense, but no one seems to await them with baited breath. I have not quite taken another lesson from Rex Stout. Before he published his first Nero Wolfe mystery, he published several turgid psychological novels no one now remembers. Once Nero Wolfe made a hit, Stout never looked back. He would write twenty of them over his career, but he also wrote Nero Wolfe novellas which first appeared in magazines and then came out in book form, in groups of three. He tried to launch another mystery series, but basically he had found his niche and did not repine. To a great degree I have accepted my metamorphosis into a mystery writer. Theron's suggestion was the best he ever gave me. The thing about mysteries is that no one is going to think you write too many of them. If they are good, that is all that matters. If it is noticed that you write a lot, well, most mystery writers do, and they don't think it a bit unusual. We have our organizations and meetings, and I have come to think that mystery writers are immune to egotism. They take their work but not themselves seriously, and they seem genuinely elated by the good luck of others, as if it's to the benefit of the whole fraternity—and sorority. Some years ago I was given the lifetime achievement award at the Bouchercon convention, pleasing confirmation that I was at home with other mystery writers.

Of the conferences put on for aspiring mystery writers, my favorites are Harriette Austin's at the University of Georgia and Katherine Kennison's at Ball State. Since I never had a class in writing fiction nor ever attended such meetings, my feelings about them are ambivalent. There are things about fiction that can be taught, but then they are easily learned by oneself. What cannot be taught are the two most important things: what you are going to write and discipline. By that I don't mean the idea for this story or that but the way one sees such imagined actions. What do they mean? This is not an abstract question. The beginning writer consciously and unconsciously mimics what he has read and liked—art imitates art—but a moment must come when his own voice emerges, his distinctive way of seeing things. For me, after many efforts, I first found my peculiar way of seeing things in "The First Farewell." I wouldn't try to define it abstractly. Others have tried, and I get a little superstitious about such descriptions. Who you are, or at least who you want to be, comes through with the stories you tell. If your assumptions are banal, received opinion, the outlook of the advertisements that flank your story, you will continue to be an imitation of an imitation. One need not be a revolutionary to have a distinctive way of seeing things that goes deeper than, if not against, the common grain. Call it the writer's philosophy.

■ As a Catholic my outlook may seem to be provided me. The believer has catechetical answers to the great questions. "What does it all mean?" becomes "Why did God make me?" Answer: To know him, to love him, and to serve him in this life and be happy with him forever in the next. Christians are supposed to imitate Christ, and presumably they all accept the truths of Christianity. If that meant that their lives must be uniform and they indistinguishable from one another, the question would arise as to why God created so many humans. One or at least a few would exhaust the possibilities of the species. The truth is a variation on Tolstoy's comparison of happy and unhappy families. The calendar of the saints tells us that the more fervently and perfectly men and women imitate Christ, the more differentiated they become. It is we mediocrities or worse who seem to blend into one another, as predictable as our bad habits. Well, the influence of one's religious belief on one's imagination is like that. All the great artists of western civilization were influenced one way or another by Christian revelation but who would confuse Dante and Chaucer, Shakespeare and Milton, Tolstoy and Dostoevsky, Hawthorne and Emily Dickinson?

All this may seem to be a presumptuous way for a minor writer like myself to view what he does. Of course when one is writing one isn't ranking oneself, only doing the best one can. I will gladly settle for being a spear carrier in the grand opera of American fiction; one need not delude oneself in order to take seriously the task of writing. What emerges will be filtered through the person of the artist. That is what the French must have meant by saying that the style is the man. It is not the goal of writing to express oneself; the self that is expressed often surprises the writer as well as the reader. But the goal is the well-made story, something with a beginning, middle, and end, a portrayal or imitation of human agents.

C. S. Lewis, who seems wiser the older I get, gave a series of lectures at Cambridge after transferring there from Oxford. These became *An Essay on Criticism.* As professor of Renaissance and Medieval Literature he wanted to reflect on the relationship between the works he studied and what people generally read. Jane Austen, when asked what she was writing, said, "Only a novel." Many readers are similarly apologetic. It is as if they wish to distinguish what they enjoy from literature. What is literature? Lewis suggests a rule of thumb. Literature is anything you would read again. There are things we would never read once, pornography, for example, but many things when read once have served their purpose. If we keep them, they gather dust on the shelf. Perhaps we trade them with others. Mystery novels would seem to be the quintessential example of the book one would not read again. Once you know whodunit, how it comes out, isn't its interest exhausted? This tells us that if story were all, how things come out, nothing would be read again except perhaps when our memory goes and then "again" become ambiguous. Books we go back to have more than plot. In the *Poetics,* Aristotle discusses that "more"— character, diction, setting, but he always insisted that plot is the soul of story. Without it, there is no scaffolding or structure for the "more" to adorn. E. M. Forster, as I mentioned earlier, toyed with the idea that one would forget all about plot if this did not turn away the groundlings— and perhaps others as well—who want a story, want to know what happens next, how it comes out.

Lewis's suggestion enables us to see, not a chasm between the great and the merely good, but a spectrum. There might even be mystery novels we would want to read again, mentioning no names. Of course it is no small accomplishment for an author to hold us for a single reading. Most writers hope to be read even if they are never reread. Lewis's rule of thumb aims not at idiosyncratic or merely personal reasons for going back to a book. I remember the delight I felt when I found *A Conrad Argosy* in a used bookstore in the very edition I had read as a boy. Such delight is only tangentially connected with Conrad—I would reread him in any edition—and doubtless we all have favorite books that are biographical rather than literary milestones.

I needed such reflections to justify my sense that what I was writing in the line of fiction, from the very beginning, was worth doing. To entertain a reader for a hour or two with a short story was no small thing. At first, of course, I had to learn the techniques required to catch and hold and satisfy the reader's interest, but from the outset there was, however faint, my own way of regarding human action. A given story is about particular actions, but one is implicitly saying something more; one's notion of what it all means, the point of deciding and choosing, of being this way rather than that, provides the backdrop for the particular story. If one made it a rule that this should always be left implicit, counterexamples would come flooding in. Imagine *War and Peace* without Tolstoy's ruminations on history and providence. More ephemeral fiction probably reinforces received opinion, and the story fits neatly into the expected. The great authors, those to whom we go back again and again throughout our lives, Shakespeare and Dante, for example, are inexhaustible. It is not necessary that we, in an egalitarian or ideological swoon, equate Fitzgerald, Dickens, Trollope, Twain, or Cather with the very greatest, nor are most of us interested in any sort of exact calibration enabling us to place precisely on the spectrum this work or that. The appraisal of fiction is not arbitrary or subjective, although there is of course the subjective, personal element when we, in the privacy of our own homes, draw up a list of our one hundred great books.

So it was all right to take up the mystery genre. Even if mysteries functioned as fictional Kleenex—one use and they're gone—the same could be said for fiction generally. Only a writer can know the depression of seeing tables of remaindered novels, the bright jackets meant to allure, the lying testimonials, but more importantly the hope and effort that went into the writing. And there they are, piled high, discounted in several senses, unwanted. That is the destiny of most books, certainly of most novels, mystery or not.

The first seven Father Dowling mysteries were published by Vanguard Press beginning in 1977. Miriam and Evelyn Schrift at Vanguard were sisters-in-law; Miriam had married Evelyn's brother. Vanguard was a family affair, having been founded in the 1930s, and including among its authors James T. Farrell, Rex Stout, Saul Bellow, and Joyce Carol Oates. Miriam was my editor, and a more scrupulous one I have never had since. She pored over the text of my mysteries as if they were high on the list of the hundred great books. This was important to me. From the very outset I dealt with people who took mysteries seriously. Miriam seemed to have read them all, and most other things beside. The two women were quite elderly when I became one of their authors. They could have been described as Manhattan Provincial. They had been outside their native city but once or twice; for that matter, they were unacquainted with most of the island on which they lived. But oh, such wonderful women they were. I must have appeared exotic to them, and when I brought my family to their offices on Madison, not far from St Patrick's, we had a regular picnic in the library, surrounded by the books the firm had published. It was always much more of a treat to have lunch brought in than to go out, with so much time then being wasted walking, dodging traffic, ordering, and all the rest. Anyone seeing Evelyn on the street, in any season but summer, would have been forgiven for thinking her a bag lady. She had a funny little helmet of a hat, with ear flaps, and she carried her work around in shopping bags. She lived in an apartment overlooking Central Park, near the Dakota building where one of the Beatles had been shot. The apartment was as it had been when Evelyn's father was alive, and its shelves featured the books that he had designed, since that had been his forte. There was help, and a man I thought of as Igor who waited on table. This was a huge piece of furniture, and there Evelyn and I would be at one end, with Igor scowling through his task. I am of course sentimental, but the Schrifts occupy a warm and permanent place in my heart.

After the Dowling series had been established, Theron Raines kiddingly said, "Now you'll have to do one about nuns." Thus was born my series featuring Emtee Dempsey. For these I used an obvious pen name, Monica Quill. They have never had the success of Father Dowling, but they have their devotees. With the advent of Sister Mary Teresa Dempsey it was established that I would publish two mysteries a year. I was also writing other things for Atheneum and then for Scribner's, but my mysteries were in the process of eclipsing those other efforts.

I was in Argentina on another Fulbright grant when I received a call from Ellen Levine, who became my agent after Theron and I amicably parted. There was movie interest in Father Dowling. But there was more. Ellen was quite upset because Vanguard had begun the movie negotiations and, as she rightly pointed out, such subsidiary rights as were involved did not belong to Vanguard. Well, everything turned out all right, but it was clear that Ellen longed to move me from Vanguard. Eventually I did move, and a blush comes to my face even now as I write that. It has been the fate of Vanguard to bring writers along and then, when they emerged from obscurity, to lose them to other publishers. The most recent case was Joyce Carol Oates. Miriam and I often talked of this. It seemed unimaginable to me that someone would leave this house. Vanguard fulfilled most of my fantasies about what a publisher should be like; its family atmosphere was an enormous plus. Everyone who worked there seemed related in some way to everyone else. However I did succumb to Ellen's arguments, and they were cogent, that it would be a smart move for me to take my fiction to St. Martin's.

Leaving Vanguard and leaving Theron Raines are the two deeds I most regret in my writing career. Theron had éclat. His offices overlooked the New York Public Library, his partner was his wife, Joan, he had the dreamy look of a man who had known many women, and he had a dog that looked like an evolutionary throwback and would drool on one's knee during discussions. Theron had been a Rhodes scholar and was in his way learned, but there came a time when his laid-back manner seemed comatose. Like most writers, I quickly became used to my good luck, thinking of it as merely part of the natural order, and hankered after more. Theron seemed undriven. And he was a fatalist. I think he genuinely believed that nothing we do can possibly influence or alter the future course of events. It was difficult to break from him. This was the man who had pulled my career out of its nadir. This was the man whose suggestion had turned me into a mystery writer. We had lunch at the Algonquin and I told him my discontents. He understood. But he wanted me to stay with him. He was almost urgent about it. I concluded that if I did, this luncheon conversation would stir him to new highs. Well, it didn't. I had agreed to stay with him another year. I did, and then I most reluctantly left him. My new agent was Ellen Levine.

When I first heard of Viacom's interest in Father Dowling I was elated but wary. *Jolly Rogerson* had been under option for years and a script had been written, but in the end nothing came of it. Of course I received something for the option, but dreams of one's story flashing across the silver screen evaporated. Perhaps this was another opportunity for dashed hopes. In the event, that didn't happen. Father Dowling was developed into a prime-time television series by the same people who had been so successful with *Murder, She Wrote.* Donald Eastlake wrote the first script. Tom Bosley played Father Dowling. It was Bosley who, more than anyone, ensured that the series had a three-year run. After the first year, the original network dropped it, but Bosley lobbied so strongly for the series that it was taken up by and enjoyed two more years in prime time on another network. Once I was listening to the Cubs and in a lull between interesting plays—there were many such lulls in those days—Harry Carey interviewed Bosley, who was there in the booth. He gave an enthusiastic plug for Father Dowling. From Rome the Nortons sent us the Italian equivalent of *TV Guide,* on the cover of which was Tom Bosley arriving at Fiumicino with a gorgeous blonde on his arm. "I'm Going To Be A Priest!" was the caption.

I had nothing to do with the series. The contract I had signed gave the rights for my characters to be developed for film and television. I myself had no interest in writing scripts. When I saw the script based on *Jolly Rogerson,* I had been struck by the vast difference between a novel and such a piece of work. It pointed beyond itself to the filming, the lines would have to be spoken, and as a script it was a remote possibility, a distant guide. Of course a novel is in a sense only potential until it is being read, but that is a self-contained transaction with the reader. More importantly, for the writer, television or studio film work inevitably is teamwork, and the writer is a relatively insignificant member of the team. One of the attractions of writing for me is that one can just sit down and do it, anywhere, anytime. It is a very solitary occupation. Even if my academic tasks had permitted joining the film team, and presuming I would have been wanted, I was perfectly content to be merely the inspirer of the series. This had the advantage of my being able to say to critics that I did not write the scripts or, to those who liked the series, to say thank you, blush modestly, and say no more. Those who had been introduced to Father Dowling on the page were more likely to object to things in the series. The great continuing advantage for me as a writer is that viewers who became acquainted with Father Dowling on television went on to read the books. The television series was a tremendous boost to my career. Indeed it continues to be. Somewhere as I write, in some language or other, episodes of Father Dowling are doubtless running on television.

The contract that I signed specified royalties per program and then a descending scale of royalties for replays. A time came when Viacom asserted that I would not be receiving royalties for replays on cable networks, that not being the sense of "replay" in the contract. There was nothing in the contract restricting the range of the word in this way. Ellen Levine deferred to her west coast counterpart. My son-in-law Paul Hark put me in touch with a Beverly Hills lawyer. After some months and preliminary exchanges, the legal advice I received was that since Viacom intended to contest my claim and since they had more money than I did, they could prolong the proceedings until *Bleak House* would look like a cabin at the beach. I am sure this was wise advice. I followed it. But it was a lesson. Imagine a behemoth like Viacom contesting with an author the mere pittance—from their point of view—of my continuing cable replay royalties and being willing to spend doubtless many times more than that in order to deprive me of what contractually they owed. I speak as one capable of understanding English sentences, not as a lawyer.

I did not repine for long. I was a writer, not a litigant. And there were books to write. The Father Dowling and Sister Mary Teresa series were now established. From time to time, in order to get out of church, so to speak, I would write a self-standing mystery—*Frigor Mortis, Infra Dig*—but I also started a third series, the Andrew Broom mysteries, the protagonists of which were an uncle and his nephew, both lawyers in a smallish Indiana town. These mysteries did fairly well. In them I was out to exploit the switcharoo to a fare-thee-well. The switcheroo—forgive the technical language—is the sudden reversal of the story so that what seems to have been happening is actually something quite different. At the outset my thought was to end each chapter with a switcheroo. Well, that would have been too much, and the series settled down into a nice comfortable niche.

Perhaps it was the economic spur that turned me into a professional writer and drove my nightly, dogged efforts in the basement of our house on Portage Avenue, learning to write publishable stories, but after I had gained my immediate objective and had us out of debt, I continued to write at what might seem a frantic pace. If I asked myself how many novels I have published, I could not answer. I do not really want to know. Consulting Amazon.com cannot give the answer, since the astronomical number of entries found by a search includes hardback, paperback, and large print editions of the same title, as well as any mention of my name on the dustjacket of another writer's book. The number could, of course, be discovered, but it does not interest me. The only novel I am interested in is the one I am currently writing.

Herman Melville's career, after knowing highs, went into decline, and he was all but forgotten when he wrote his late novel *Billy Budd*. In his portable writing desk there was found a motto: Be true to the dreams of your youth. I like to think it sustained him as he wrote on in undeserved obscurity. Finally, that is what any writer does, return again and again to the original aspiration that came to him when young. It is the writing, producing a well-made story, that counts. All the rest is gravy.

SEVEN

LEARNING HOW TO DIE

SOCRATES SAID THAT PHILOSOPHIZING IS LEARNING HOW TO DIE. This was not a mordant statement, because one can learn how to live humanly only when one has come to terms with the fact that death is certain. When Albert Camus said that the first philosophical question is whether or not to commit suicide, since asking any other question presupposes that this one has received a negative answer, he can be seen as drawing attention to the normally unquestioned good of being alive. News? Not at all. A good deal of philosophy is a matter of articulating what one already knew, what everyone knows, implicitly at least, the way we know without thinking about it that it is good to be alive.

I was introduced to philosophy by way of Aristotle and Thomas Aquinas. Only later would I realize what an enormous advantage this was. Aristotle and Thomas were realists. They thought the human mind was a capacity to know the world and ourselves, the way things are. Your grandmother thought the same thing. Alas, one of the dominant assumptions of modern philosophy, beginning with René Descartes, is that prior to getting her mind rinsed in methodic doubt your grandmother cannot truly say she knows anything. The philosopher now looked with skepticism on the wisdom of the race. It all seemed unwarranted, dubious, even manifestly false. One could not build on such a foundation. One must first sweep it aside and replace it with something so clear and certain no one could doubt it. Then we could go on.

Now there is something to be said for this, of course. There is a lot of nonsense that becomes received opinion. For example, that a mother has the right to abort her baby thanks to her claim to privacy. Or that smoking cigarettes is a crime against humanity punishable by expulsion into the winds of winter, to stand huddled in a corner, sinning by inhaling. Or that people thought the world was flat prior to Columbus. Common sense may seem a lot of nonsense. But to conclude from this that ordinary people do not know lots of things for sure is quite a jump. When playing with kids you say, "Inchme and Pinchme went out in a boat. Inchme fell in, who was left?" Until the child realizes that the only answer he can give will earn him a pinch and buttons his lip, he has shown that he knows, without knowing it explicitly, perhaps, that $(a + b) - b = a$. And he knows that when equals are taken from equals, equals remain. (Not that sentence, perhaps, but what it means.) More fundamentally, he knows the tongue twister that expresses the most basic truth about reality, thinking, and talk: "It is impossible for something to be and not to be at the same time and in the same respect." The first time one hears that it sounds like "Peter Piper picked a peck of pickled peppers." But what it says, no one can fail to know because we all know it before hearing or formulating the sentence.

Aristotle and Thomas looked for such certainties embedded in common speech, graspable by everyone, unlearned, except in their reflexive formulations, those tongue-twisting sentences. I have come to think that there is only one basic difference that divides the tribe of philosophers into two camps. On the one hand, there are those philosophers who see what they do as a continuation of the kind of thinking everyone engages in, a continuation that can get progressively more recherché but, if it cannot be taken back to its common origins, can be assumed to have gone off the track. On the other hand, there are those who see philosophy as providing the absolute starting point of thinking; nothing worthwhile precedes it since nothing that is not the product of formal philosophizing can be credited as knowledge. Most philosophers nowadays fall into the second camp. It is this that has made philosophy seem a jargon, a game played with decreasing seriousness by those who make a living at it.

Not that anyone is particularly happy about the dominance of this second way of viewing philosophy. From Descartes on, the history of philosophy can seem like a series of efforts to overthrow one's immediate predecessor as well as the tradition he overthrew. Philosophy in the modern age is constantly trying to make itself over, to find the right method, the correct starting point, the juncture where things went wrong. The most fateful feature of the critical turn has been to introduce a chasm between thinking and its presumed object, the world out there. Sometimes we are deceived by our senses and think straight things are crooked, so how can we be sure that what we are thinking matches anything out there? Philosophical sanity requires that one does not let this problem arise because as such it is insoluble. If, as the problem suggests, we are first aware of our thinking and must then go on to relate it, truly or falsely, to something beyond thinking, we will never escape the realm of thinking. That is why it is so important to see that this problem is based on a false assumption. That is, it does not arise.

To doubt everything is impossible. *De omnibus dubitandum est*, as Kierkegaard showed in a little unfinished work of that title, is a project that cannot be carried out. And yet, as his Johannes Climacus was told, this is the starting point of philosophy. So on that basis philosophy could never begin. Of course the flaws in the claim to universal doubt are part of the lore of philosophy, but not everyone who sees those flaws takes the obvious next step, that since we cannot always be deceived, there are things about which no one could be deceived. That is, certain knowledge is presupposed by philosophizing and not its gift to the world. By contrast is the view that our knowledge bears on things, not as they are, but as we know them, making the relationship between ideas and that of which they presumably are the ideas increasingly problematic. No wonder philosophy over the last century has seemed to reel from one form of self-assertive subjectivity to another, with its last state being skepticism that there is anything beyond our construals to know anyway. Truth along with objectivity goes out the window.

■   This is a big bold sketch of the discipline into which I was introduced. My first instructor in philosophy, as I have described earlier, was Father William Baumgaertner at St. Paul Seminary, fresh from receiving his doctorate at Laval and with all the enthusiasm of a teacher at the dawn of his career. For logic, we read books of the Organon of Aristotle, aided by Thomistic commentaries. For metaphysics, we read in Aristotle's eponymous work while Baumgaertner put the apparently disparate parts into a coherent whole. We were not detained by the still flourishing notion, put into currency by Werner Jaeger, that the treatises of Aristotle, especially the *Metaphysics,* were not literary wholes but a more or less happenstance collection of Aristotle's lecture notes, dating from many periods in his life when, allegedly, he held different opinions. If that were true, obviously commentaries that drew attention to the order and development of the fourteen books of the *Metaphysics* must seem fantastic. In the case of Thomas, who commented on the first twelve books, not only are the books in the right order in relation to each other, but the chapters are wonderfully ordered, and within each chapter yet more marvelous order can be discerned. With other teachers, as I have mentioned, I read textbooks—Brennan's psychology manuals with Father Larry Wolfe and Joyce's *Natural Theology* with Butch Baskfield—another Butch. Ladislaw Sledz taught us the history of philosophy from a text by Turner, his predecessor in the post. Sledz had been caught in Poland when the Nazis invaded from one side and the Russians from the other. He was imprisoned. Somehow he escaped and ended in the aula maxima at St. Paul Seminary, trying desperately to reconcile explanations of Empedocles and Heraclitus with the hell he had been through. There was something called an education course, which was about what you would expect, and biology. Our professor came over from St. Thomas College, and the subject was so exotically different from anything else on the curriculum that we loved it. The professor was a great showman. His course provided an opportunity to ask the kind of question you couldn't ask in moral theology, say. The topics of human reproduction, the formation of the baby, birth, led someone to ask, "What does it feel like to have a baby?" There were only men in the aula. The professor was a man. He squinted at the questioner, thought, then said, "Have you ever shit a football?"

The transition from Nazareth Hall and the almost exclusive emphasis on language and literature to the St. Paul Seminary and its almost exclusive emphasis on philosophy should have been more difficult, but from the outset I was hooked—for life, as it was to turn out. "All men by nature desire to know." Thus Aristotle begins his *Metaphysics* and then goes on to develop the implications of that truism, one of the most important of which is that the thirst for knowledge can only be assuaged by such knowledge of God as we can acquire. Soon I found myself sought out by fellow students to explain what we had learned in class. A year or so ago I got a letter from Jim Stonich, in retirement in Joliet, where he had served as a priest. It began by saying that he would probably have become a truck driver rather than a priest if I hadn't convinced him that the problems he was having with philosophy were superable. I found I couldn't remember the avuncular lecture I allegedly gave him, another of those occasions, more often unsettling, when others remember what we do not. In this case I was happy to take whatever small credit for saving the nation's highways from a driver meant to become a priest. Priests are notoriously reckless drivers and not, as a wit has supposed, because in their case a priest does not have to be sent for in the event of an accident.

I became so enamored of philosophy in my first year at St. Paul's that soon Father Baumgaertner and I were talking of the possibility of my attending summer school at Laval. A LaCrosse classmate, Norman Senski, also decided to go, expressing quite explicit plans for eventually obtaining doctorates in both philosophy and theology and teaching one or both. Perhaps the encouragement I received would have led to my being selected for advanced study after ordination. When I returned in the fall and reported to my new residence, Father David Dillon received me warmly, saying, "I understand you spent the summer in Quebec." He said this almost conspiratorially. He was another doctor of theology from Laval, a tall redhead of enormous dignity and grace. His stately progress from his rooms to the lecture hall, with a volume of the Leonine edition of the *Summa theologiae* under his arm, was a sight to behold.

In Quebec, Senski and I had rooms in the Grand Seminaire, a forbidding edifice next to the cathedral. Classes were in a building on the Chemin Ste-Foye, and this entailed that we walk from the old town, out the Porte St. Jean, and on toward the Faculté de Philosophie. Here was the *fons et origo* of everything that had won me to philosophy in St. Paul. First and foremost, there was Charles De Koninck, then in his mid-forties, dean of the faculty and the best Thomist I ever met. That, of course, means the best philosopher. It would become a common libel after Vatican II to say that Catholic philosophers who took their lead from Thomas Aquinas were hopelessly narrow and provincial, closed off from the exciting world of modern thought. I will come back to this. If a way of doing philosophy is to be assessed, it is only right to assess it in terms of its strongest, not its weakest, exponents. That there were many second-rate, even third-rate Thomists I have no doubt. But the same can be said of the exponents of any identifiable current of thought. No one who knew the work of a De Koninck, a Jacques Maritain, or an Étienne Gilson could fail to see the falsity of the criticism. Their reputations and influence were not confined to their fellow Thomists but met with respect throughout the philosophical world.

Summer lectures at Laval were by and large in French, though De Koninck taught one of his in English, as did Charles N. R. McCoy. For the French, I was lucky to be included on a list of recipients of carbon copies of notes taken by a woman with stenographic ability and a good sense of what she was recording. With these notes supplementing the class, I could concentrate on attuning my ear to philosophy in French. M. l'abbé Maurice Dionne taught that summer, though he was an infrequent attender of his own class, as did Jacques de Monléon from the Institut Catholique in Paris. The story was that de Monléon and De Koninck had arrived in Quebec to claim the same job and that de Monléon gave way to De Koninck because of the latter's already burgeoning family (Charles and Zoe De Koninck would eventually have twelve children, the last born just before my first). Even I could detect the difference of quality in de Monléon's French. He lectured with bemused distraction, sometimes lifting one foot off the ground and holding it suspended as he marshaled clauses into beautifully complex sentences that seemed pellucid. Sometimes it seemed that he might lift the other foot as well and float ethereally around the room, lecturing all the while. But the champion of the endless sentence was Aurèle Kolnai, who once allegedly gave an hour-long lecture that consisted of a single unbroken and grammatically correct sentence. Kolnai, I was to learn, was out of sympathy with the Laval method of concentration on texts of Aristotle and Aquinas. Later I took from him a course allegedly on the *Politics* of Aristotle, in which he endeavored to disprove all the claims of that work. Need the good ruler be a good man? Kolnai asked, mischievously lauding the role that Rasputin had played in Russian governance. My friend George Lavere, who had come to Laval from Toronto, took Kolnai for his mentor, wanting to be something of a rebel even in paradise. But that was later.

In the Grand Seminaire, where Senski and I were housed, the doors closed for the night at nine o'clock. Seminary discipline is fine, but we were on vacation and soon began to kick against the goad. It wasn't that anyone was keeping an eye on us. One day we found our way into the attic of the building and came upon great quantities of the proceedings of the Canadian Thomist society. Two of them contained contributions by Charles De Koninck, so we took a copy of each. Perhaps the rest of them are still there, undisturbed after more than a half century. It was the closing of the doors of the seminary so early in the evening that we were determined to circumvent. We did this by leaving unlocked a window in the scullery and, having exited the building, sliding under a back gate, where years of usage had created a kind of tunnel. We would lay newspaper, lie down, and zip, we were on the town. Mainly what we did is just wander around, enjoying the crowd, but eventually we would stop for a beer. Drinkers put up two fingers when they ordered, saying *"Deux fois."* They did not want to wait for that second beer. Beer came in liter-size bottles, so, having followed the custom of the country, we returned to the seminary in a pleasant glow. Under the back gate, into the scullery, up the stairs, home free.

The rooms were austere, the refectory was austere, the whole place was austere. I had yet to read Willa Cather's *Shadows on the Rock,* but when I did, her seventeenth-century Quebec could easily be imagined from memories of the seminary. By contrast, St. Paul Seminary seemed a country club. Senski, who was studying for the LaCrosse diocese, after two years in St. Paul, importuned his bishop to send him to Quebec to complete his studies. Here was a man who had decided to design his own future. *Cada uno es artifice de sa ventura* might have been Senski's quixotic motto. If so, God is not mocked. His plan was to be on the spot in Quebec, to add courses in the Faculté de Philosophie to his seminary theology courses, and to have at least a licence in philosophy when he was ordained, perhaps also the doctorate. Then he could turn to theology and get another doctorate. Even if this plan had worked out, which of course it didn't, it was difficult to know what purpose all these advanced degrees would serve in LaCrosse. When I came to Quebec in the fall of 1952 I would see Senski from time to time, scooting back and forth to the seminary from classes. His ambition was undulled but things had gone, if not agley, not smoothly. He was still there, with a year to go to ordination, when I left with my doctorate in philosophy. He would be assigned to the minor seminary at LaCrosse, which was all there was, and years later would leave to teach at Santa Barbara. I met him at a meeting of the American Catholic Philosophical Association, where he told me this. So far as I know he published nothing, which, for an ambitious man, was odd. He dropped from sight, like Browning's Waring. The last I heard he was teaching in one of the municipal colleges in Chicago, the academic pits, and had made the *Wall Street Journal* when margin calls revealed that he been playing fast and loose. What's become of Senski? God knows, and that's the important thing.

■   In 1951 I left the seminary, certain at last that I was not meant to be a priest. It was more or less by default that I enrolled in graduate school at the University of Minnesota. My big plan was to get a degree from Laval, but in the meantime Minnesota was a target of opportunity. Minnesota was then on the quarter system, which is ideal for students, since the same amount of material is covered as in a semester course and you have the chance to take lots of different courses, which is what I wanted. That year I took, *inter alia,* four courses from Wilfrid Sellars and four from Paul Holmer. The courses by Sellars were on Descartes, Leibniz, Kant, and his own theory of knowledge. Sellars was the son of Roy Wood Sellars of the University of Michigan, who won a deserved niche in American philosophy but always resented the assumption that the Ivy League schools were by definition better than such a place as Michigan. Wilfrid Sellars had an Oxford M.A., had come to Minnesota from Iowa, and together with Herbert Feigl edited one of the best compilations of the kind of philosophy they both did, variously called logical positivism, logical empiricism, and, later and more vaguely, analytic philosophy. Sellars wore dark suits and light brown shoes and glided back and forth before us as he talked, a sort of slinky sentry walk. He wore a mustache and there was always at least the beginning of a smile on his face. In one of his courses he distributed offprints of an article of his own, "Some Aristotelian Philosophies of Mind." Among other things, the article discussed thirteenth-century interpretations of *On the Soul,* Sellars favoring the Averroistic interpretation of intellect against the Thomistic. I seized on anything that could link what I was now doing with the philosophy to which I had been introduced. Unlike most philosophers of his persuasion, Sellars was knowledgeable in the history of philosophy. The papers I wrote for him were often efforts to compare what he was saying and what I imagined Thomas Aquinas would say. This, along with my use of the phrase *tout court* in a paper, caught his attention, and he called me in for a chat. I suppose I must have looked like a laboratory specimen, a throwback. He was not at all condescending, but his recurrent point was that my outlook could not withstand the turn into modern philosophy. Read Hume, he

Birthplace, February 24, 1929,
at 36th Avenue,
South Minneapolis.

1931, after my long blond
curls were cut off.

From left to right:
Roger, Austin, Raymond,
Mary Margaret, myself, Dennis,
and my mother in profile.

First Holy Communion,
with my mother, May 10, 1939.

Nazareth Hall, Lake Johanna.

Library at
Nazareth Hall.

Connie and I
on our wedding day,
January 3, 1953.

Holding Michael in our
apartment at 60 Avenue des
Braves, Quebec, 1954.

Charles De Koninck,
my mentor,
Doyen of the Faculté
de Philosophie,
Université Laval,
Quebec.

Instructor in
philosophy,
Creighton University,
Omaha, 1954–55.

On board the *Statendam* in 1959, en route to Louvain as Fulbright Research Scholar. In Louvain I would write my first book, *The Logic of Analogy* (1961).

On the English Channel in 1970, smoking mandatory pipe and wearing a Notre Dame windbreaker.

Sacred Heart church on the campus of
Notre Dame, 1966. Arnold McInerny
is among the fallen World War I
alumni commemorated there.

Passport picture, 1969.
In front, from left to right:
David, Beth, Daniel;
in back, Mary, Cathy, and Anne.

Connie and I welcoming a new book, 1975.

Connie and I
in the yard at
2158 Portage Avenue,
South Bend.

From left to right: Marvin O'Connell, Liz Christman, myself, and Tom Stritch, 1980.

Arrival of bust of Jacques at the Maritain Center.
From left to right: Father Hesburgh, Connie, Jean Oesterle, and myself.

Castel Gandolfo, with Pope John Paul II; Louis Dupré at my right.

Honorary degree,
St. John Fisher, 1996.

The Michael P. Grace
Professor of Medieval
Studies, taken in the
office of the Maritain
Center, 1996.

Connie revisits the Atlantic Building in Louvain. Our apartment was on the fifth floor in 1959–60.

Festschrift dinner, 1999, with Father Hesburgh and Jude Dougherty.

Professor Dr. Astrik Gabriel, my predecessor as Director of the Medieval Institute and scholar extraordinary.

Connie and I with our six children and then sixteen grandchildren, with Father Hesburgh.

With Alice Osberger, celebrating her twenty-five years as administrative assistant of the Maritain Center.

Three philosophical friends: John Haldane, Dave Solomon, and Tom Hibbs.

Laura Bush, myself, and daughter Mary at the White House, 2004.

Marvin O'Connell and myself after more than sixty years of friendship.

Portrait of an author, 1997.

advised. Read Locke. In later years, when he was famous, having taught at Yale and then at Pittsburgh, and becoming ever more obscure in search of clarity—among other things, he had three different ways of quoting, using single quotes, double quotes, and dot quotes—he always regarded me as one of his students and was unfailingly kind. When he spent a week lecturing at Notre Dame, he gave my colleagues the impression that we had once been thick as thieves. I am deeply grateful for the chance to study with him.

Years earlier, David Swenson had found a copy of Kierkegaard's *Concluding Unscientific Postscript* to the *Philosophical Fragments*, in Danish, in a used bookstore in Dinkytown, a little enclave of bookstores and restaurants on the edge of the campus of the University of Minnesota. (It was so named because dinky little engines used to pull cars from there into Minneapolis proper.) Finding a Danish work in Dinkytown was plausible because of the number of Scandinavians in the area. Swenson devoured the book and subsequently translated both it and the book to which it was a postscript into English. In discovering Kierkegaard, Swenson had found his way, philosophically. Paul Holmer was in a direct line to Swenson. Holmer had gone off to Yale to study, working with Ernst Cassirer. When Cassirer died, the only copy of Holmer's dissertation in progress was impounded with Cassirer's papers. Holmer then wrote another, on Pascal and Kierkegaard, and joined the faculty at Minnesota. He was a big, broad-chested man with thick glasses, thin blonde hair, and a ready laugh. He became my mentor. To have been introduced to Kierkegaard by Holmer was a grace. Besides a course on Kierkegaard, I took one on Cassirer, another on Karl Jaspers, and another in philosophy of history. I would learn that Holmer was an ordained Lutheran minister, as was the venerable old man of the department, George Conger. Protestant seminarians in the area often enrolled for Holmer's courses. I would write my master's dissertation under his direction.

May Brodbeck taught logic, using Quine's *Methods of Logic*, which begins, "Logic is a very old subject, and since 1879 it has been a great one." I was fascinated by propositional calculus but found that I had to drive from my mind any question as to how this related to the logic I had learned in the seminary. Fell swoops and full sweeps, and other Quinean devices, could be learned like games and enjoyed accordingly. This was not a course in philosophy of logic, except in tendentious asides, but the assumption was that in mathematical logic we had the instrument philosophy had been in search of. Come to think of it, I did read Bertrand Russell's *Philosophy of Logical Atomism* with Sellars. Logic was described as a beautiful language; all it lacks is a vocabulary. The idea was that the variables in logical forms could take any values and yield certainty in any area. How something got to be a variable of x or y or z was a problem, of course. Russell pondered long and wittily over "The king of France is bald." How parse it, there being no French king? Russell's solution was that molecular propositions were broken into atomic ones, ϕx, say, in which something was attributed to something. But predicates in atomic propositions had to be the most basic things in the world. These, Russell held, were sense data. A later and sassier version of this that we read was A. J. Ayer's *Language, Truth and Logic*. Ayer was twenty-five when he wrote this work, so of course he knew everything. It was now clear that symbolic logic had become a Procrustean bed. What didn't fit was lopped off by being declared meaningless. So few years after all this, it has come to seem quaint. The celebrated Principle of Meaningfulness—that a term had significance if and only if it took a sensory object for its meaning—and the Principle of Verifiability—that a proposition could be accounted meaningful and true if and only if it matched some sensory fact—fell victim to their own assertion. That every term must mean something sensed and that truth consists in the one-to-one correspondence of the elements of a proposition and the elements of the corresponding fact render these very claims meaningless.

The propositional logic I learned defined the truth of molecular or compound propositions as a function of the truth of their constituent atomic propositions, so that the analysis of the former into the latter was the path to verification. Russell's logical atomism identified atomic propositions as reports on sense data—for instance, "red patch now"— and molecular propositions as compounded of them. Claims and assertions that could not be verified by thus analyzing them into atomic propositions expressive of sense data were dismissed as meaningless. Ayer cheerfully brushed aside all moral, theological, and aesthetic affirmations as meaningless. That this renders 99 percent of what we say meaningless delighted rather than dismayed him. But soon all this fell victim to its own principles.

In some respects, modern philosophy can be described as the Reformation carried on by other means. It can certainly be described in terms of a series of turns. The first was the turn to the knowing subject and the quest for a method of thinking that would guarantee the grasp of truth. But by making ideas the primary object of thought, an unbridgeable gap was created between thought and any object beyond thought, giving rise to a series of systems culminating, perhaps, in that of Immanuel Kant and reaching its apotheosis in Hegel. For Hegel the problem was solved by identifying thought and being, thus eliminating any need for relating the one to the other. The so-called linguistic turn was taken when the notion of an inner world of thought was replaced by the quite public function of language. Ludwig Wittgenstein is the patron saint of this turn, and his influence has been enormous. Wittgenstein, an Austrian who came to England to study but returned home to fight in World War I, left the army with the only book he published in his lifetime, *Tractatus Logico-Philosophicus*, the burden of which could be said to be to show the inanity of philosophical problems. After Wittgenstein's death everything but his Baby Book was published—the Blue Book, the Brown Book, and many more—and they spawned many incompatible interpretations of what he had meant. Wittgenstein was the Ezra Pound of modern philosophy: if Pound in the *Cantos* tried to mimic the fragments of Sappho, Wittgenstein seemed to be producing pre-Socratic fragments. One of the more charming schools was that of so-called ordinary language philosophy, with J. L. Austin as its most influential member. Early in the century G. E. Moore had written "A Defence of Common Sense" against idealism, which was reminiscent of the great Scottish philosopher Thomas Reid's common sense philosophy meant to refute the skepticism of his countryman David Hume. Such defenses have an inescapable realist ring to them— that is, take as given that we know such things as that snow is white and water is warm and this is to know things about snow and water—and so it seemed to the ordinary language philosophers. But despite Moore's effort, ordinary language philosophy has been eclipsed by the most radical turn of all, that which attributes to language what Kant and Hegel attributed to thought—any extralinguistic reference is ruled out, language is sufficient unto itself, it does not stand for something outside it. Languages are the work of communities, of course, and it may thus seem that those who speak the same language are in some kind of agreement about the way things are. Obviously this is not so.

This is an impressionistic, thumbnail sketch of what was considered the mainstream of philosophy to which I was introduced at the University of Minnesota. It consigned the philosophy to which I had been introduced in the seminary and would continue to study when I went on to Laval, to the margins, the swampy shorelands, the defunct. At this point I suppose I should say that some of my best friends bob around in this mainstream, occasionally coming up for air, being carried around one turn and another. Needless to say, they have always seemed to me to be in trouble and I myself to be standing on firm ground. If this were merely an autobiographical fact, a statement that while some, perhaps most, philosophers go at it one way, I go at it another, the whole thing would seem arbitrary. All of us might then simply seem to be products of the way we were introduced to philosophy in the first place. That is why I have always considered it a friendly duty to point out that those in the soi-disant mainstream are not philosophizing in an alternative and legitimate way but are involved in a deep incoherence, and not just from some other and alien point of view, but on the terms they themselves accept. By contrast, the way I do philosophy is not just a way of doing philosophy, it is philosophy. And it isn't my way, it's ours. Perhaps the most annoying claim of all is that those who allegedly reject this common wisdom of the human race surreptitiously invoke it, thereby displaying that they have not hit upon some radical alternative to it. I wonder if I would have seen this if I had not begun the study of philosophy in the seminary. I doubt it. But then it is less likely that I would have gone into philosophy anyway. An introductory course in philosophy, just about anywhere over the last fifty years, would have sent me fleeing.

■ It was by contrast with the alternatives that the thought of Thomas Aquinas became even more attractive to me than it had been. Now I understood the point of a title of one of Jacques Maritain's earliest books, *Antimoderne.* Contemporary philosophy was a disaster area. No wonder the Church had pointed to Thomas Aquinas as the principal mentor in philosophy as well as theology. A glance at the efforts which characterized the first phrase of the Leonine Revival initiated by the 1879 encyclical *Aeterni Patris* shows how unerringly the neuralgic point of difference was recognized. Modern theories of knowledge had to be confronted because if they were viable the whole edifice of classical philosophy would have been shown to be built on sand—a point, of course, made by modern critics of that tradition. This zeroing in on the theory of knowledge—words like criteriology and epistemology came into vogue—had a tendency to skew the principles of classical philosophy. Étienne Gilson had a point when he objected to the primacy of a defense of realism, critical realism, since this seemed to concede that knowledge was primary and our capacity to know the real problematical rather than self-evident.

When I returned to Laval in the fall of 1952, I was eager to immerse myself in the alternative to what I had learned at the University of Minnesota. During that Minnesota year I had heard Charles De Koninck when he came to St. Paul to lecture and saw a living model of what I wished to become. Like Jacques Maritain, De Koninck was a layman. He was also married and the father of a large brood. Although he had been born in Belgium, he spent boyhood years in Detroit before his parents returned to their native Belgium. He was educated in Belgium, tried a vocation in the Dominicans, and when that proved not to be his destiny, took his degree in philosophy from Louvain. Shortly thereafter he came to Quebec, where, young as he then was, he was soon the acknowledged star of the Faculté de Philosophie. In the summer of 1950 I had already followed his courses, but then I was a seminarian, and he could not be an exact paradigm for me. Now he was.

De Koninck was a short, plump man who sat when he lectured, beaming at his audience, on the alert for the response to what he said. He ended almost every sentence with an interrogative "eh?" He once wrote that his ambition was simply to be a faithful student of his master Thomas Aquinas. Discipleship seems to have either of two results. The disciple never emerges from what the master had accomplished and is content to retail it. Or, and this was the case with De Koninck and other giants of the Thomistic Revival, Thomas was followed because his starting points were the inevitable ones, and by acknowledging and seeing where they led, one could go far beyond the text of the master while at the same time claiming that what one said was simply an organic extension. It is only in this second way that a tradition can live. And Charles De Koninck was the liveliest Thomist I have ever known. One of his interests was Marxism and sovietology, and when Roosevelt and Stalin met in Quebec, De Koninck thought there should be a debate on Marxism with the Soviet dictator. Surely a discussion of Marx and Engels would have made more sense than discussing the Four Freedoms with one of the greatest butchers of the twentieth century. *Notre critique du communisme, est-il bien fondée?* provides some flavor of how such an exchange might have gone. De Koninck, for all his accomplishments, died young, at the age of fifty-eight, while in Rome advising his bishop at Vatican II. He was found dead in his room in the Columbus Hotel on the Via della Conciliazione. I have felt his loss ever since, but this has been mitigated by the marvelous work of his son Thomas.

I have already indicated the exiguous finances on which we lived in Quebec. As a result, I went through there like a bullet, as I had at Minnesota. Taking the master's in a year was technically possible, but no one did it. When I sat for my comprehensive writtens, I scarcely recognized anyone in the room. They had been boning up for a year for the exams. I was in a hurry, and Paul Holmer, initially surprised at my intention, supported my effort to wrap it up within a year. I wrote my master's dissertation with him, a presumptuous effort called *A Thomistic Evaluation of Kierkegaard*. I went home to marry Connie on January 3, 1953, took my licence in philosophy in 1953, and received my doctorate in 1954. When I talked to De Koninck about doctoral dissertation topics and he learned about my master's dissertation, he urged me to continue working on Kierkegaard, thus saving me from writing on Kant, as I had originally proposed to him.

But it was of course the classes at Quebec that occupied me principally. The method at Laval was almost exclusively to read the texts of Thomas, and this meant chiefly the commentaries on Aristotle. This was exactly what I wanted. The approach was ahistorical; little attention was paid to the setting in which the works had been produced, as would have been the case at the Pontifical Institute of Mediaeval Studies at Toronto, where Gilson was the guiding spirit. Despite what might seem the limitations of the method, I have become more and more convinced over the years that the Laval approach was the best, certainly the best for me. De Koninck and the others seemed to have every line of Thomas at their fingertips, as a television evangelist has the Bible. The analogy does not limp. We read Thomas as an all but sacred text, forming our minds, becoming Thomists of the strict observance. Not that our professors were disinterested in the relevance of Thomas to what had happened since, but one had to go to their published writings for this. The classroom was where one concentrated on Thomas; only when Thomas's thought had become second nature would comparisons be possible. (I winced to think of my master's dissertation.)

De Koninck himself had developed a philosophy of science that argued for a continuity between the philosophy of nature as begun by Aristotle and the latest developments in physics. This view had developed from an early influence of Maritain, only to become an alternative to it. While he wrote much, De Koninck was a sprinter rather than a long-distance runner. There is no book of his that is not manifestly a compilation of shorter pieces. There is no definitive statement of his views on the relationship between philosophy and science, although *The Hollow Universe* contains the elements. The massive dissertation by Bernard Mullahy, C.S.C., directed by De Koninck, can be taken as that statement. De Koninck directed many dissertations, some of them becoming almost joint works of his and the candidate's. For the most part, he published his pieces in the *Laval théologique et philosophique*, sometimes short and sometimes very long. He was also interested in theology, principally Mariology—he had a doctorate in theology as well as philosophy—but often he would publish in such places at the Quebec clergy review. Career management was not uppermost in his mind. He resisted offers to go elsewhere, preferring the relative isolation of Quebec if only because it provided an ideal environment in which to raise his family. He traveled much, however, lecturing throughout the United States and Canada; the extra income was not unimportant for his domestic economy. Although there is a significant body of written work and many of the lectures found their way into print, De Koninck's principal influence on me was person to person. The better I got to know him, the more I admired and wished to emulate him.

During the summer of 1953, I was hired by the university to work in De Koninck's study to put order into his papers. This was largely an excuse to provide me an income, I think, but every day I would show up at his house on the Avenue Ste Genevieve and settle down in his study to rifle his file cabinets and read his books—he had an enormous and impressive philosophical library. He wrote his first drafts in longhand and then gave them to a typist, who made at least two carbons. Folders in the cabinets thus always had the ribbon copy and at least one carbon. Nervily, I asked him if I could take carbons of his stuff. Of course. Thus I amassed a cache of DeKoninckiana. Among his papers were lecture notes of his courses, and of these too there were often carbons. This was a tremendous bonus of that summer. I don't know if I put much order into those file cabinets, but I certainly lightened their burden. One day I came upon what seemed to be an attempt to write a novel. It was pretty bad. During that summer I also came to know his wife, Zoe, and his oldest child, Thomas, who was to become a lifelong friend. I am now engaged in the task of producing an English collected edition of the writings of Charles De Koninck, a task prompted by both *pietas* and gratitude.

Among my fellow students in those days were Sheila O'Flynn and John Warren. John would marry Sheila's sister Nancy, and Sheila, who came to St. Mary's College in 1956, would marry Joe Brennan of the Notre Dame English department. After an interval devoted to her children, Sheila joined the Notre Dame philosophy department. In the early 1960s, Charles De Koninck became my colleague at Notre Dame, spending the fall semester there and living with John and Jean Oesterle, both of whom had studied with him in Quebec. It was a heady moment when I first addressed him as Charles.

■   After my single year at Creighton University, I came to Notre Dame. It was 1955. We were all Thomists of a sort, with Louvain and Toronto and Laval well represented. Perhaps the only non-Thomist was Bob Caponigri, who had studied with Richard McKeon in Chicago. Bob was a polysyllabic philosopher who, while he may not have sought obscurity in what he wrote, usually attained it. A reviewer of one of his books, having praised it, added that he thought Caponigri had not been well served by his translator. There was no need of a middleman to achieve the obliquity of Bob's style. Father Herman Reith was chair of the department when I arrived; Bill Roemer, a gentle and diffident man, was the senior faculty member, although of course everyone seemed old to me. Father Leo Ward was sui generis. He had been instrumental in bringing Yves Simon to Notre Dame, but by the time I arrived Simon was teaching at the University of Chicago, though he kept his Notre Dame residence and continued to be a presence among us. One evening at the Oesterles, he and De Koninck vied with one another to establish their peasant origins, a bit of a Romantic effort in both cases.

Connie and I were closest to the Oesterles, but Vincent Edward Smith, whose doctorate was from the Catholic University, and his wife, Virginia, also became very close friends. When Vince left Notre Dame in 1959 to accept the directorship of an institute at St. John's University in Jamaica, New York, for, if I remember correctly, the then astronomical salary of $15,000, all the Smiths in their new station wagon stopped at our place on their way out of town. To me the thought of leaving Notre Dame was inconceivable, but in the case of Vince Smith it approached the impossible. While I was at Creighton, after I had accepted the offer to come to Notre Dame, I drove into Iowa to hear Vince lecture. In the course of it, he spoke of the feeling he had each morning turning onto Notre Dame Avenue and seeing the statue of Our Lady atop the golden dome of the Main Building, visible through the trees that flanked the road. He spoke with such feeling, with such identification with the university, that I could not believe it when he decided to leave. He had been there since 1950. I suspect that he left because a colleague had written a private estimate of the department dismissing Vince and John Oesterle as anachronisms. And Father Innocentius Bochenski had been rude to him, chiding him for arriving late for his course, which Vince was sitting in on as a courtesy to the visitor. Eventually Bochenski insulted everyone. Many years later, entering a bookstore in Paris, my eye was caught by the cover of a book featuring the unmistakable bullet head of Bochenski. He seemed to be trying to smile for the camera, but his expression still looked like a scowl. The book, which I bought, was a translation from the Polish of interviews he had given in Poland. Of course I was interested to see what he would have to say about his time at Notre Dame. All he remembered was what he had done, and Ivo Thomas, another Dominican whom he regarded as his protegé. For the rest, it was condescending. I was not surprised.

I will not call the roll of the department of those days, but I must mention some other names, first of all Joe Bobik, who arrived at the same time as I did. We swiftly learned we were kindred spirits. Joe had taken his doctorate at Notre Dame, writing with John Fitzgerald, and after teaching in California and at Marquette University, had come home. John and Pat Fitzgerald became close friends with whom we often played bridge. Herb and Nell Johnston were also bridge players. There was another John Fitzgerald as well, who became my golf partner, but he eventually went off to a campus of the University of Massachusetts. A couple years after I joined the department, Ken and Lucile Sayer arrived. Ken had been recommended by Henri Dulac, who had met Ken when on a fellowship at Harvard. And of course there was Ernan McMullin, from Donegal, Ireland, with a degree from Louvain. He had come in 1954, recommended by the Oesterles, who had met him in Louvain when they were there on a Fulbright. Those were the days of what came to be called the Old Boy Network. Bochenski, who was a visitor at Notre Dame during my first year, would also be the patron of any number of my future colleagues.

On occasion I have made lists of those who spent some time at Notre Dame and then left. Since leaving Notre Dame has been inconceivable to me since I first arrived, I am always mystified when others depart, for one reason or another. When I depart it will be into that bourne from which no traveler returns. It makes little sense, no doubt, but I have always taken the fate of Vince Smith as cautionary. Soon after he settled in at St. John's as the director of an institute devoted to the philosophy of science, he stepped down as editor of *The New Scholasticism* and John Oesterle took over as editor, with myself as associate editor. The idea was that the journal of the American Catholic Philosophical Association should continue to have the éclat of being located at Notre Dame. It was Vince who said this. I went out to St. John's to consult with Vince during the transition. He was well located, he and Virginia now had a house in Jamaica, close to the campus, and in many ways all looked well for them. It was the lull before the storm. Soon afterward, agitation arose at St. John's, with Father Peter O'Reilly, another former colleague at Notre Dame, as chief agitator. O'Reilly was a priest of the Chicago archdiocese and a Torontonian Thomist of the strictest persuasion, who at Notre Dame had taught an introductory course to graduate students, stressing his own very Gilsonian Thomism. When, as the youngest member of the department, I had been assigned the task of keeping notes of the departmental meetings, I once wrote, "as Father O'Reilly wryly observed. . . ." I was soon relieved of the task. O'Reilly had an apartment over Woodward's Bar on Eddy Street, where the cards on which he was recording an index to the *Summa contra gentiles* accumulated. In those days before computers, such a task was pursued in a way indistinguishable from the way a medieval scholar would have proceeded. Living where he did, O'Reilly acquired an undeserved reputation as a free spirit. As it happened, he nursed the notion that he had a vocation to the Carthusians, and the time came when he resigned and went off to the monastery. Within months he had changed his mind, but when he sought to return to Notre Dame he was told that his position had been filled. This could not have gladdened his heart. He taught for a while at Xavier in Cincinnati and then went on to St. John's in Jamaica and the turbulence of the early 1960s.

At St. John's, Vince Smith was in the unenviable position of not wishing either to align himself with the rebels or to dissociate himself entirely from their grievances. He compromised by teaching his classes in his home while his colleagues boycotted the campus. This had the predictable effect of alienating both sides. But much worse was to come. Virginia was killed during a break-in in their home, wholly unrelated to the campus commotion, and a few years later, Vince himself was struck and killed by a cab on Park Avenue. The whole thing had the look of a Greek tragedy, from which I drew the personal and irrational moral, Beware of leaving Notre Dame.

Some years later in the *New York Times,* Peter O'Reilly's engagement was announced under the headline, Songbird of the Bronx to Marry Peter O'Reilly. The reference was to a newspaper poetry contest his fiancée had won when she was a girl. The photograph of the prospective bridegroom might have been his ordination picture, with black suit and Roman collar. He ended his career in California.

■ Pre-conciliar Thomism is a fascinating topic, one I have discussed in my 1966 book *Thomism in an Age of Renewal.* There are certain givens in the discussion. The first is that Thomism of various kinds was dominant in Catholic colleges and seminaries, thanks to the Leonine Revival. In Jesuit colleges, the number of required courses in philosophy was enormous. When I came to Notre Dame from Creighton and found that there were only four philosophy courses required for graduation, that seemed minimal to me. What were the courses? Logic, philosophy of nature, philosophy of man, and metaphysics. That ethics was not one of the required courses became an object of discussion, and for a time we agitated for an additional course. While this discussion was going on, I ran into Father Hesburgh on a campus walk, and after the usual pleasantries the question of that added course came up. Father Hesburgh wasn't against it, exactly, but he offered an analogy. When someone came to him and asked for instructions in the faith, they might have months, even a year, to devote to this. Or it could be far less time. A few weeks. And, in the crunch, it might be that one would have to meet the request then and there. His point was that the truth can be tailored to the time one has to convey it.

I liked that analogy. And notice that the assumption was that our way of doing philosophy aimed at truth. We were not merely acquainting students with what a lot of people had written or said. We addressed fundamental questions and proposed answers to them on the basis of argument. Did one become a logician as the result of a three-credit course? Perhaps not, but one learned what an argument is and how to avoid fallacies, which is no small thing. Did one come into possession of a proof for the immortality of the soul? Did a student emerge from metaphysics capable of proving the existence of God? Putting such questions reminds one of the ambiguities of teaching and learning. It is always a good question what exactly one learned over the course of years of study. Who, ten years later, without review, could formulate, let alone defend, a classical proof for God's existence? One of the things that happened during the Council was that questions like these began to express a radical discontent with what we were doing. Was not our instruction more catechetical than philosophical? What value was there in being able to rattle off certain formulas if it was simply rattling off? Slowly such discontents took the form of a critique of Thomism. There grew in the minds of many the thought that exciting things were being done in the philosophical world and yet there was no place for them in our curricula. Oh, one could offer a course in contemporary philosophy, but this made the discussion of Kierkegaard and Marcel seem marginal.

This discontent soon became fueled by the conviction that the Fathers of Vatican II had deliberately dethroned the thought of Thomas Aquinas. It was no secret that foes of Thomism were among the *periti* at the council. That Thomism had lost its hegemony was never a question of appeal to conciliar documents. Like so many other convictions that swept through Catholic institutions in the mid-1960s and afterward, this was attributed to the "spirit" of the council. This was what I discussed in *Thomism in an Age of Renewal.*

For some the book retains an evocative effect, but for most today it describes a situation they did not personally know. When I look at it, I realize that I did not in my heart of hearts take very seriously the arguments that were flying about. I still don't. It is salutary and necessary to appraise what one is doing as a teacher, and it is well to realize how modest are the results of one's efforts. Particularly when one is young, the efforts of colleagues can seem to fall woefully short of adequacy. With the first fervor long since gone, people go on teaching without great enthusiasm. Nor can it be stated too often that nothing detracts from the interest of a course for most students than the fact that it is required. To face twenty-five or thirty students who have not chosen the course you are teaching but need its three credits to graduate is not the ideal setting for addressing ultimate questions. This is the main reason that, for better or worse, higher education has become a matter of auto-design by students. The materials are set before them, and they can arrange them pretty much as they wish.

Let me address this first of all. When the required courses in philosophy fell from four to two, there was no diminution in the numbers of students who signed up for philosophy courses. This seemed a good argument for the free market. In the years since, with registration taking place by computer, it has become clear that students who select courses on the basis of the hour and days they are offered soon find that their first choices are foreclosed. Others have gotten there before them. What next? Second choices, desperate stabs, who knows? To some degree we have come full circle. A professor can face classes of students many of whom, perhaps most, are there because they could not get into the class they wanted. In order to ensure competition, restrictions are put on the number of students who can take a course, sometimes as few as fifteen. Clearly the idea that students can choose their courses is an ambiguous claim. This is a small point, but important to make, since criticism of what we had was usually accompanied by utopian visions of the alternative.

Some of the animus against Thomism arose from the sense that we were caught in a medieval time warp, while elsewhere exciting things were being thought and said. There was human respect involved in this; there was also a looking to the neighbors in a way that would come to characterize and caricature the suburbanite. Many were simply embarrassed to be thought Thomists. Did this follow from the growing conviction that Thomas Aquinas was wrong on this or that or the other thing? Were detailed critiques forthcoming on the errors of Thomism that induced one to abandon his allegiance to Thomas and place it elsewhere? These are, of course, rhetorical questions. I believed then and believe still that the vast movement from the ranks of Thomists was brought about by shallow motives.

Perhaps the greatest irony stemmed from the fact that the Thomistic Revival had been based on the judgment that wrong turns had been taken in modern philosophy, turns which were leading, and now had led, to disastrous intellectual, social, and cultural results. Thomism had not been proposed by Leo XIII as just one way of doing philosophy among others which he chose arbitrarily to champion. Thomas stood for a way of doing philosophy whose principles were radically opposed to the principles of modernity. The Spirit of Vatican II sought to undo this judgment. The

Thomist critique of modernity was embarrassing. Many wished to make their peace with the epistemological turn taken with Descartes.

And, as it turned out, one could do this and call it a species of Thomism. So-called Transcendental Thomism, that of Joseph Maréchal and Karl Rahner, called for a rereading of Thomas that would bring him into line with modern assumptions about the primacy of thinking. For many, this began a journey that ended with Heidegger. Others became enthralled with phenomenology, whose slogan, "To the things themselves," seemed to call into question the modern assumption that thought, not things, was primary. But whatever the reason, most of those who abandoned Thomism turned to existentialism and/or phenomenology. Very few found analytic philosophy attractive. This had odd consequences. The dominant mode of Anglo-American philosophy, outside our own institutions, was analytic philosophy. Here and there, at the University of Buffalo, at Northwestern University, there were phenomenological pockets, but these were regarded with amused disdain by analytic philosophers. Thus it was that many Catholic philosophers fled from what they regarded as the Thomistic ghetto, only to find themselves in a phenomenological one.

I am being cynical. If one changes one's philosophical stripes out of conviction and on the basis of analysis or argument, so be it. One might quarrel with the analyses and arguments, but the exchange would be of a philosophical sort. As the hegemony of Thomism melted away, however, one was not confronted by devastating critiques that explained the departure. It was largely a matter of mood. Bob Parelat taught at St. Mary's College and was a ferocious Thomist of the existentialist variety. For him, the thought of Thomas not only could be but should be severed from that of Aristotle. During my first years at Notre Dame, we had memorable marathon discussions, neither able to convince the other of our respective position. Well and good. One day, after the turmoil of the Council, Bob came to me with the astonishing announcement that he was through being a Thomist; he was going to become an analytic philosopher. He was going to immerse himself in Russell and Moore, he would read Wittgenstein, he would pore over *Mind.* What had brought this about? He had yet to immerse himself in the writings of those to whom he intended to devote himself. This immersion was meant to be the alternative to and rejection of Thomism. Having studied these thinkers myself and having decided that they were scarcely on the level of Thomas Aquinas, I was astonished. Dramatic as this instance was, I think it was more typical than not. Vatican II had that sort of effect on many.

■ When I was hired at Notre Dame, the chief reason was that I had written dissertations on Kierkegaard. I was a Thomist but with interests in existentialism, particularly of the Kierkegaardian variety. During my first semester I was asked to speak to my colleagues on Kierkegaard, and in the second semester Father Leo Ward arranged for Fred Crosson and myself to give public lectures on phenomenology and existentialism. The assumption at the time was that members of the department shared a core commitment to the thought of Thomas Aquinas but were interested in relating it to other things, to developments in science, in logic, in philosophy of religion. Our departmental aim—in many respects it was simply the intention of the Thomistic Revival—was to develop a new Thomism that would incorporate whatever truths could be found anywhere and to mount criticisms of faulty positions. This was not a department which seemed vulnerable to the conciliar malaise about Thomism. Nonetheless, there was a failure of nerve, often justified by self-criticism of our efforts. The self-criticism normally would have been healthy but now seemed an argument for changing our fundamental aims.

Change, even of the most basic sort, is often imperceptible to those caught up in it. Our department changed under the pressures of the post-conciliar mood, but there was never a moment when anyone proposed a radical change. What were proposed were modifications of our effort. I do not mean the kind of criticism Ernan McMullin had made of Vincent Smith's philosophy of science. This was the kind of difference one expected among philosophers, who could be presumed able to handle criticism. Vince Smith and some others, however, had had a decisive impact on the entire college curriculum. In the grips of the notion that there is a proper order of learning the philosophical disciplines, on which our required courses were based, syllabi were worked out for these courses, and instructors in them met regularly during the semester to discuss their common effort. Father Sheedy, the dean, once said to me that on any given day he knew exactly what was being taught in any class of the college. It should be said that this organization was not confined to philosophy, but philosophers had sought to arrange other disciplines with an eye to their relation to philosophy. This, more than anything, made many ripe for the abandonment of required courses.

Many of my new colleagues were chosen because they brought to the department knowledge of something going on in contemporary philosophy that the rest of us did not share. Ken Sayer brought from Harvard a competence in epistemology, Harry Nielsen was a Kierkegaardian Wittgensteinian. (It was at his home that a group of us read *Philosophical Investigations* when it first appeared.) Nick Lobkowicz was an expert in sovietology, Guido Kung in the relation between analytic and continental philosophy. Some of these new colleagues exemplified the older pattern and were versed in Thomism, others did not. That some among us did not share the presumed core commitment was thought not to be troublesome. There was no hostility yet to the common commitment.

Over time, of course, this is what brought about the change in the department. People were hired because of the competence they had without any reference to a departmental commitment to the thought of Thomas Aquinas. As the years passed, the department came to consist of a variety of philosophical viewpoints without any serious way of relating them to one another. This had dramatic effects on our undergraduate program as well as our graduate program. Eventually departmental meetings came to resemble a session of the United Nations without interpreters. If anyone had proposed a definition of philosophy or a statement of what we were doing as a group, it would never have been adopted.

Many consider this parlous situation as simply a phase in the change of the department toward some presumed standard model. The department, like the university, has become obsessed with rankings. Rankings are of course made on the basis of criteria. One seldom hears a discussion of the criteria, so enamored have we become of the results of their application. But surely to rank high on some criteria is to have failed on others. Once there was the notion that doing philosophy in a Catholic way not only answered to an urgent cultural need but also put one into the tradition that stretched back to the dawn of western civilization. Modernity had sought to rupture that tradition, to cancel the past and start anew, with terrible results for society as well as philosophy. The Thomistic Revival was the embodiment of that conviction. Needless to say, secular philosophers did not at first share that negative estimate of the quasitradition in which they stood. But in recent years nothing has become more commonplace than the assertion that the Enlightenment has been a failure. The promise of endless progress following on liberation from all external constraints sounds hollow against the history of the twentieth century. Something went wrong. A not untypical statement of this is George Steiner's *In Bluebeard's Castle*. A dramatic version of the problem is the death camp commandant listening to Bach with tears in his eyes. Clearly the notion that education and culture would lead to moral betterment is dubious. Newman had pointed out as much in "The Tamworth Reading Room." So what is the solution? Steiner toys with the idea of a religious explanation but dances away from it. In the end, he suggests hope stemming from the computer.

This habit of prescribing more of what has caused the problem is a mark of our age. Philosophers, aware that something has gone wrong in their discipline, do not see the need for a 180-degree turn. What are considered radical solutions merely plunge us deeper into nihilism and relativism. In short, the culture and its philosophy have grown worse since 1879, and the remedy Leo XIII proposed remains the only cure. The human mind must again be measured by reality rather than make futile attempts at the reverse. How ironic that Catholic philosophy since the Council has taken on the coloration of modernity and all but abandoned its traditional roots. Our departments of philosophy now have a majority of members for whom what I have been saying would be as unintelligible as doubtless it would be at Meatball Tech. It is a melancholy thought that now, when the salutary impact of traditional philosophy is most urgently needed, we who are its presumed representatives have abandoned ship and are crowding the rails of the Titanic.

EIGHT

NOTRE DAME

TOM SCHLERETH'S 1976 BOOK ABOUT NOTRE DAME PRESENTS THE campus as a kind of palimpsest, later times laid upon earlier, so that if you take the walking tours he recommends you find yourself peering beneath the present to a past that is somehow still there although gone forever. Alumni, faculty, staff, those whose lives have been lived at Notre Dame, if only for a time, have their personal palimpsests. One who like myself has inhabited these coordinates of space for half a century can sometimes feel the campus is haunted as persons and events are evoked by a building, by a path along the lake, by a vista that suddenly brings the past rushing in on one. Of course Schlereth is presenting more than the memories of those still living; he is presenting a history of the phases whereby a log structure by a lake improbably gave rise to what we partisans regard as the premier Catholic university in the United States.

In a remarkable short story, "Harv is Plowing Now," John Updike locates the memory of a devoted and dutiful son at the bottom geological layer of the narrator's self, the point of reference which enables him to assess his later actions, usually finding the comparison to Harv a moral rebuke. Harv is remembered as plowing perfect and regular furrows in the field across the road, and the man's continuing role in the narrator's moral assessments of himself is captured in the title of the story. We all build up the self we are, layer on layer, seldom consciously, so that later events evoke earlier, and we are awed by our mysterious continuity in time.

■ In August 1955, I drove our Hudson to the campus for the first time, and when I came along Notre Dame Avenue toward the dome I was reminded of Vince Smith's description the previous spring. He had spoken so movingly of his morning walk to campus up Notre Dame Avenue, seeing before him the great pile of the Main Building with its golden dome, atop which was a massive statue of Our Lady, the patroness of Notre Dame du Lac. I was coming home to a place where I had never been. I parked behind the law school and walked onto the main quad. Turning to the east, I saw O'Shaughnessy Hall, then but two years old. I can remember as if it were yesterday, in the phrase, walking toward the entrance of O'Shaughnessy, entering, climbing the stairs to the third floor, and going along it until I found the joint offices of the Philosophy and Religion departments. No one was there. This was August, the lull between the ending of summer school and the beginning of the fall semester, then in late September. It didn't matter. I was just getting my bearings.

I suspect that everyone who loves Notre Dame remembers his first sight of the place. Father Hesburgh once said an outdoor Mass where the quad that runs from O'Shaughnessy to Rockne meets the other that moves south from the main building. I think this was part of the sesquicentennial celebrations in 1992. Speaking from the improvised sanctuary that faced south, Father Hesburgh was suddenly reminded of the first time he had come down that road onto campus. He spoke of it both matter-of-factly and movingly, I suppose because he knew that each of us had such a memory.

The history of Notre Dame is not encompassed by any living memory, of course, and memories are incorrigibly personal. Both Tom Stritch and Ed Fisher wrote of their times at the university, but each memoir was more than autobiographical. Still, somewhat as with the space of the place, our memories are laid upon the past. A time comes in anyone's life at Notre Dame when he becomes curious about its unexperienced past. Sometimes it comes too late. It is possible for a student to dwell on campus for four years and have almost no sense of what went on here before he came. When I was asked to develop a mystery series that would have the campus for its setting, it occurred to me that this gave me an opportunity to make some bit of local historical lore integral to the ongoing story. Thus, in *On This Rockne*, I had the plot turn on the novel that the legendary coach published in 1925, *The Four Winners*. I had often surprised people by mentioning this novel, and had a personal reason for not wishing it to fall into oblivion.

In my first year at Notre Dame, I shared an office in the main building, next to the student prefect's, where every morning delinquents sat on a kind of mourner's bench in the hallway waiting to be called in and scolded for some transgression or other. I shared the office with Willis Nutting, Phil Gleason, and Henri DuLac. It was a high-ceilinged, dusty place, with a few old desks and older chairs, and an unrivaled view out the single window of an airshaft. Andy Warhol would have been inspired by the wall of bricks that met the eye across a few feet of space.

In one corner of the office, there was a massive metal door, which opened onto a safe built into one of the pillars that support the dome. One rainy day, Willis Nutting and I opened the door and rummaged around in the safe. On a shelf were a number of packages. We felt them. They had the feel of books. We took one of them into the office and opened it and copies of Rockne's novel spilled out on the desktop. Now Willis, about whom more later, was the sort of professor who seemed never to have noticed the football stadium, and he was amused by this revelation that Knute Rockne had actually written a novel. I chuckled along with him until I opened one of the copies and saw the dedication. "To Arnold McInerny, Member of the Notre Dame football team. Killed in action at Château Thierry, July 1918. A man whose loyalty to his school, to his friends and his country, whose gentlemanly conduct, scholarly attitude, courage and conviction, and high sense of honor make him an ideal of which Notre Dame is justly proud." Well. Suddenly, although the newest member of the faculty, I felt related by blood to the history of the place. It was a solemn moment.

Despite that dedication, Arnold McInerny is little more than a name now. He is listed on the commemorative plaque to be found on the east door of the Basilica of the Sacred Heart under the legend "God, Country, Notre Dame." I have tried to find out who he was, without success. Not even Kevin Cawley in the Notre Dame archives has been able to resurrect Arnold McInerny. However extraordinary Knute Rockne found the man, he has disappeared into that great anonymous crowd of our predecessors on this campus. God knows them all by name, but history keeps a more fitful record. Without some knowledge of that history, we will be like those barbarians—our ancestors, that is—who swept down on a Rome known to them only because of its waning military might. In Africa, St. Augustine, who had taught in the Roman Rhetorical schools, saw the lights of Europe going out as a result of the waves of invasions. And so they did, to be relit gradually and over centuries while the great classical patrimony was laboriously rediscovered and preserved in monasteries, culminating in the universities that spread over the continent beginning in the thirteenth century.

■ Father Edward Sorin, member of the still new Congregation of Holy Cross founded in France by Basil-Antoine Moreau, had been sent in his twenties to the New World and, after a sojourn in southern Indiana, came north in 1842 to claim the land that would become the University of Notre Dame. What are now two lakes was then one—hence the singular *du Lac* in the French title of the university—it was winter, the arrival has passed into legend. On the shores of the lake, the newcomers took up residence in a primitive structure. Marvin O'Connell has written the life of this extraordinary man who is our founder, and his book came as something of a revelation to a community whose collective memory had grown dim. Sorin kept a chronicle during the first dozen years or so, in French, and it was brought out in English by Father James T. Connolly as part of the sesquicentennial celebrations. It is written in the third person and conveys the incredible hardships of those first years, as well as the profound piety and devotion of the founder. There were squabbles between the New World foundation and headquarters in France, and a time came when a decision was made to break free of the home community. A representative of Moreau arrived. Sorin was about to go down and give him the news. And then, suddenly, he fell on his knees and prayed, reminding himself of the obedience he had promised on joining the congregation. When he went down to the superior's representative, it was to proclaim his fealty. I have often thought that was the moment when the future of Notre Dame was providentially assured.

We need a history of the university of the caliber of O'Connell's life of Sorin. When it is written, such men as John Zahm will emerge as the giants they were. (He figures in *Irish Gilt*, one of the mysteries I have set on campus.) Father Daniel Hudson, the longtime editor of *Ave Maria,* a magazine that had a tremendous influence on American Catholicism, will also loom large. Father Sorin was ever attracting new people to his growing university. Maurice Francis Egan, whose house, The Lilacs, still stands on Notre Dame Avenue, was a colorful figure, professor of literature, novelist, eventually American ambassador to Denmark. Sorin tried to bring the nineteenth-century controversialist Orestes Brownson to Notre Dame, but in the event the great man arrived three years after his death, to be buried in the lower church in Sacred Heart. The inscription on the stone beneath which he lies in the main aisle has been almost worn away by the shuffling feet of communicants. Arthur Schlesinger Jr.'s Harvard senior essay became what remains one of the best introductions to this fascinating man.

Notre Dame, despite its location in the wilds of northern Indiana, had a national presence of varying degrees from the beginning. But what propelled it to the forefront of Catholic universities was Knute Rockne and the Fighting Irish. Rockne's unexpected victories over national powerhouses elevated Notre Dame to undisputed prominence in athletics. Across the country, Catholics who had never seen the campus became as it were default alumni. That the team was called the Fighting Irish suggests the upward mobility that was involved in this turn of events. Anyone who remembers the contempt and condescension with which Henry Thoreau refers to Irish laborers, or the much less excusable snobbery of William Dean Howells, attitudes indicative of both racial and religious prejudice (even though traces of it are to be found in the Catholic novelist F. Marion Crawford as well), will appreciate that a gridiron victory by Notre Dame meant far more than a gridiron victory for American Catholics. And the success of Notre Dame athletics created conditions for strengthening the essential, academic work of the university.

■   During the half century I have been at Notre Dame, the university has made enormous strides in its quest for excellence. When I came, it was of course much smaller than it has become, with a student body half its present size and with fewer than half the buildings that now fill the campus. Priests of the Congregation of Holy Cross, wearing their habits, were everywhere, although from its beginnings Notre Dame had prided itself on the number of laymen on the faculty. The president was Father

Theodore Hesburgh. (There have been only two presidents during those fifty years, Hesburgh, and Monk Malloy, whom I had as a student when he was a seminarian.) Not long ago, I met Father Hesburgh, coming from the residence in which he occupied a simple room like any other priest, about to walk along a lake path. He suffers now from macular deterioration, an affliction he bears without complaint. He can no longer read, and it is only because he knows the prayers of the canon of the Mass by heart that he can continue to celebrate in the chapel in his retirement suite of offices on the thirteenth floor of the Hesburgh Library named for him. When I told him the sad news of Connie's illness, his first impulse—we were in the library—was to say, "Come upstairs. I'll say Mass for her." And so he did. I read the Scripture passages and served as altar boy while he offered the sacrifice of the Mass as he had done every day since his ordination.

For people my age—and there aren't many left—Father Hesburgh has been a reassuring symbol of continuity throughout the many dramatic changes at Notre Dame during the past half century. He is rightly called the second founder of the university. He is one of the few genuinely great men I have known. Now that Father Edmund Joyce is gone, I tell myself that if I should survive Father Hesburgh and Father Herman Reith, who was chairman of philosophy when I arrived, I will indeed feel on the precipice separating time from eternity, with no older folks obscuring the view. I don't think we fully appreciate what the loss of Father Hesburgh will mean to Notre Dame. No longer will the new be buffered by his solid reassuring presence. I suppose that sort of vertigo was felt when Father Sorin died.

■   In 1955, Father John Tracy Ellis, an historian at the Catholic University of America, published an article which subsequently became a little book in which he cast a baleful eye on Catholic higher education. Its poor performance was gauged by applying a number of criteria, among them the presence—or absence—of Nobel Prize winners on our faculties. Ellis urged a new striving for excellence. Ellis's argument was one that fitted perfectly into Father Hesburgh's hopes for the university. A great new effort—there had been several such in the past—to attract to the faculty scholars of national and international prominence got under way. Monsignor Philip Hughes, the Church historian, came, and Boleslaw Sobicinski, who would found the *Notre Dame Journal of Formal Logic*, there was

Waldemar Gurian, who founded *The Review of Politics,* Stephen Kertesz and Gerhart Niemeyer in government, Otto Bird, first director of the General Program in the Liberal Arts, Yves Simon, Vincent Smith, Charles De Koninck and Father Bochenski in philosophy, Ivo Thomas the logician, and many more. This effort was in full swing in the postwar years, during Vatican II and its immediate aftermath. Great things happened.

In many respects, the effort was a continuation of the upward mobility that had been represented by the surprising fortunes of the football team. The prominence the university had gained in athletics was now regarded, however, with something akin to embarrassment. During these years, I gave a lecture at Ohio State which I began by saying how delighted I was to be in Columbus since I had always wondered what a football factory looked like. Polite laughter, but then I was speaking to medievalists. In my own way, I suppose I was conveying the sense that Notre Dame was now striving for academic excellence first of all.

The Church in America has always been driven by the desire to figure prominently and equally in the American scene. Tocqueville, in his discussions of religion in this country, made the surprising prediction that the land would end up either all Catholic or all pagan. Since he was a bit of a lapsed Catholic (though he died an edifying death), this cannot be ascribed to partisan motives. When Tocqueville wrote, Catholics were a negligible part of the national population, but with the waves of immigrants that soon changed. A dispute arose among German and Irish Catholics, the former more wary of assimilation in this country of Protestant origin (as long as one forgot the French and Spanish), while the Irish under the redoubtable John Ireland, archbishop of St. Paul, were determined to become part of the national mainstream. (Marvin O'Connell has written a life of Ireland as well as of Sorin.) Rome shared the misgivings of the non-Irish, and a heresy called Americanism was condemned. Well, assimilation has always been a tricky business, for Catholics as well as Jews, and ambiguities if not dangers became clear in the drive for academic excellence.

■   A simplistic formula for making it (the allusion to Norman Podhoretz is intended) in the American university scene would go something like this. The criteria of excellence are embodied in the great schools of the Ivy League. (Only Laval in Quebec is a Catholic institution of equal age, and it had little influence on American higher education until the middle of the twentieth century.) Both academic and social prestige are defined by the Ivy League. Any institution of higher learning that seeks excellence should, accordingly, model itself on the Ivy League. Thus it was that young members of the Congregation of Holy Cross were sent off to Yale and Harvard and Princeton for advanced degrees, or even to Vanderbilt. New faculty were recruited from those with Ivy League degrees.

Now this may sound like, if you can't beat them, join them, and to some degree that is what it was. What tended to be forgotten in the discussions stirred up by the Ellis article was that Catholic universities stood in the mainstream of western culture. Only such forgetfulness could explain the question: Can a university be great though Catholic? The flip remark that a Catholic university was a contradiction in terms was too often heard. Only someone ignorant of the history of universities could ask such a question. The first universities of Europe had all been Catholic institutions. On the continent, Reform and Revolution had altered that, but in England Oxford and Cambridge continued to be religious establishments, which is why John Henry Newman lost his fellowship when he converted to Catholicism. When he was named rector of the Catholic University of Ireland and delivered the lectures that became *The Idea of a University*, he dreamed of an institution that would reflect the Oxford from which he came and return the ideal to its original inspiration. Prior to Ellis, Catholic institutions had looked to Newman's great work for guidance. That now was in danger of being forgotten.

One of the insufficiently noticed dangers in taking the Ivy League as model was what had happened to most of those universities. Almost all of them had begun under religious auspices, but that was now becoming a fading memory, no longer operative in those institutions. What came to be called secularization was taking place. The Notre Dame historian George Marsden, a Calvinist, had recounted the abandonment of their original inspiration of universities founded by Protestants, and James T. Burtchaell, once provost at Notre Dame under Father Hesburgh, in his magisterial *The Dying of the Light*, had extended the story to include Catholic institutions. Hence the great paradox of Catholic universities like Notre Dame taking their cue from institutions which had begun as religious foundations but were no longer guided by their founders' ideals. Did the quest for excellence entail the secularization of Notre Dame?

■ What was the alternative? As it happened, during the years just before I came and afterward, a number of Notre Dame professors had written about the direction the university should take in the future. Willis Nutting, after his conversion to Catholicism, came to Notre Dame precisely because it differed from the secular milieu in which he had been educated. Notre Dame was different. It could of course be better, but amelioration lay in strengthening the things that made it unique. Benedict Ashley became a Catholic while at the University of Chicago and immediately decided that he should continue his studies at a Catholic institution and where better than Notre Dame? His was one of the first Ph.D.'s awarded in political science—his dissertation dealt with Aristotle's concept of natural slavery. He then entered the Dominican Order, and I came to know him when our philosophy department met twice a year in Chicago with colleagues from Marquette, Loyola, De Paul, and the Dominican House of Studies at River Forest, where Ashley then was.

Leo R. Ward, C.S.C., published *Blueprint for a Catholic University*; in the prospectus Ward drew up for the graduate program in philosophy, the stress was on bringing Yves Simon to Notre Dame. Rufus Rausch and the legendary Frank O'Malley devised a Philosophy of Catholic Literature program in the English department; Rausch as a student had picked up G. K. Chesterton in Niles, Michigan, and driven him to the campus. John T. Frederick, a non-Catholic, had a profound influence on the way literature and writing were taught at Notre Dame. Frank O'Malley's notion of how Notre Dame could become more Notre Dame, that is, more Catholic, is conveyed in a number of powerful essays. (Frank served as editor of *The Review of Politics* for a time.)

These are but a few indications of the treasures contained in the past of the place that could influence reflections on your future. One could go on contrasting the road not taken with that we have actually been traveling over the past decades. The comparison is not, of course, between the good and the bad. Who knows what an untried alternative would have led to? And who would deny the many gains that have been made in going the way we have? But perhaps we stand now at a kind of crossroads. As we move into the presidency of Father John Jenkins, we have an unequaled opportunity to assess where we have been and where we are going. It can sometimes seem that in recent times we have regarded our commitment to Catholicism as sufficiently fulfilled by the liturgical celebrations that take place on campus—in Sacred Heart, in the chapels in each of the residence halls—as well as in the stress on public service which is concentrated in the Center for Social Concerns and the work of Holy Cross Associates. These are necessary conditions for a Catholic university, but they are not sufficient. They go on elsewhere than on campus. Our essential university task has to do with the life of the mind and imagination, with what goes on in classrooms and theaters and literary publications. What I fear is the seemingly growing belief, expressed more in deeds than in theory, that the academic disciplines are or ought to be unaffected by the religious commitment of the university. But wouldn't it be odd if history and economics and political science, to say nothing of philosophy, were taught in a way that was indistinguishable from the way they are treated everywhere else? It would be equally odd if scientific research was uninfluenced by the moral and religious convictions of Catholicism.

Think of these as clouds on the horizon rather than any adequate description of what does go on in our classrooms. To the degree that they represent dangers, proximate or remote, surely the remedy is to foster a robust sense of the pervasive importance of the faith. As the earlier allusions to the history of universities were meant to suggest, this is not a proposal for radical innovation. Our philosophy, our literature, our music, our art, our architecture have over the centuries been developed in the ambience of the faith. The great triumphs of western culture bear the unmistakable mark of the faith. They constitute our patrimony as well as a challenge as to how we should distinctively proceed into the future. We all need models for our work. Surely there are more appropriate ones to be found in our tradition than in the secularized culture around us. Pope John Paul II, in *Ex Corde Ecclesiae, From the Heart of the Church,* recalls the faith's essential role in the rise of universities and appeals to Newman for guidance as to how we can best serve our mission. So too, his *Fides et Ratio, Faith and Reason,* deals with what from the beginning has been the central task of the university, to bring into harmony the truths of faith and those attained by reason.

Nor are such models to be found only elsewhere and long ago. The history of Notre Dame is rich in provocative instances of how we should advance. We owe it to ourselves to reflect on the remarkable career of John Zahm, the range of his interests, his intellectual liveliness informed by his faith. He was a scientist. He was philosopher and theologian. He was a lover of Dante whose acquisitions form the basis of our remarkable Dante collection. The Jacques Maritain Center is a continuing tribute to one of the most comprehensive Catholic thinkers of the twentieth century, the range of whose interests and competence is truly amazing. In the future, the Maritain Center under John O'Callaghan, the Center for Ethics and Culture under Dave Solomon, the Nanovic Institute for European Studies under Jim McAdams, and the Erasmus Institute could well serve a special role in recovering and correcting and inspiring Notre Dame's efforts.

Notre Dame athletics continue to provide a point of reference and a caution. In December 2004, Tyrone Willingham was summarily dismissed as head football coach. Not even Gerry Faust, with his disappointing record, was let go before his five years were up, but Willingham was fired after three. The search for his successor was demeaning to the university. The impression given was that the first item on the agenda of the incoming president was to hire a winning coach. The *New York Times* asked me to write an op-ed on the matter, and after some hesitation I agreed. I have no desire to make public criticisms of my university, but public acts sometimes demand a public response. The unseemly flight to Utah to make an offer, just days after firing Willingham, was doubly so because it was unsuccessful. In the event, Charlie Weis was hired for two million dollars. Two million dollars. The rule under Father Hesburgh had been that no coach would earn more than the highest paid professor. I have been told that Ara Parseghian's top salary as football coach was $35,000. It will be objected that, despite the upward climb of professorial salaries, this rule would effectively relegate Notre Dame to amateur status. 'Tis a consummation devoutly to be wished. Any one who requires two million dollars to come to Notre Dame should be wished well in his future endeavors and forgotten.

Consider this analogy. Each year lists of the prime high school prospects for college football are published and all the major football programs go in pursuit of these lads. Including Notre Dame. There is no reason to think that those whose names are on such lists are apt prospects for the University of Notre Dame. They are wooed and won basically on the grounds of whether a program will facilitate their entrance into professional football on graduation. Is that the purpose of Notre Dame football? Are our athletes to be primarily athletes and incidentally Notre Dame students rather than the reverse? Better to settle for inter-hall football than that. The irony is that under this new professionalization, fewer rather than more of our football players are drafted into the NFL. If that is to be a consideration, we seem to have done better by proceeding in a specifically Notre Dame manner. Ara Parseghian chose his players on the basis of a personal interview in which he sought to find out what was in their head, what was in their heart, what was in their soul. In short, were they potential Notre Dame men. If they did not pass that interview, he did not care if they could run like the wind and otherwise excel athletically. Romanticism? Look at his record.

And what is the analogy? In hiring new faculty, we should make a similar assessment of how a future teacher will fit into the Notre Dame ideal. There may be uniform criteria for appraising athletes—although they will not exhaust the criteria for bringing someone to Notre Dame, if Ara Parseghian is right—but I doubt that there are uniform criteria for academic excellence. There are criteria, however, and they are quite objective. But a man or woman could satisfy those criteria, or a subset of them, and still not be an apt addition to the Notre Dame faculty. What is in his or her head, certainly, but more importantly, what is in his or her heart and soul?

Well, call these the ruminations of an old professor in the twilight of his career who loves Notre Dame, warts and all. This institution does not exist only in the present moment. It draws on the historical capital symbolized by the graves in the community cemetery, where, in a kind of clerical Arlington, under identical crosses, lie the deceased members of the Congregation of Holy Cross. And in Cedar Grove, on Notre Dame Avenue, lie professors and their wives. One can walk there and conduct a kind of posthumous faculty meeting. There would be no present if it had not been for the efforts of our departed brethren.

Charles O'Donnell, C.S.C., the poet president of the university, long ago wrote his "To Notre Dame." I will adopt it now as my own farewell.

> So well I love these woods I half believe
> There is an intimate fellowship we share:
> So many years we breathed the same brave air,
> Kept spring in common, and were one to grieve
> Summer's undoing, saw the fall bereave
> Us both of beauty, together learned to bear
> The weight of winter:—when I go otherwhere—

An unreturning journey—I would leave
Some whisper of a song in these old oaks,
A footfall lingering till some distant summer
Another singer down these paths may stray—
The destined one a golden future cloaks—
And he may love them, too, this graced newcomer,
And may remember that I passed this way.

Notre Dame

NINE

VATICAN II

IN HER NOVEL *THE MAN ON A DONKEY*, H. F. M. PRESCOTT RECOUNTS in the form of a medieval chronicle the passage in England from Catholicism to a national church, showing the confusion and ambiguity that attended that change. Any Catholic who was raised prior to the ecumenical council held in the early 1960s and then has lived most of his life in the post-conciliar Church will feel an odd affinity with the characters of Prescott's novel.

Pope John XXIII, seemingly surprising even himself and certainly everybody else, called the council, and its first session—there were to be four—convened in St. Peter's Basilica in 1962. When the council closed on December 8, 1965, Pope John was dead—he died after the first session— and it fell to Paul VI to promulgate the sixteen documents which the council fathers had produced. Before he died, particularly from 1968 onward, Paul had become a tragic and beaten figure who once suggested that the smoke of Satan had crept into the Catholic Church. One can compare that somber sentiment with the exuberant optimism with which John opened the council. In his opening address, good Pope John decried the prophets of gloom, suggesting that all was well with the Church. And with the world? Well, the former must open its windows to the latter, the apparent prediction being that renewed energy would flow from the secular into the sacred realm. John did not envisage a council of the usual sort, when serious doctrinal disagreements had to be settled; his was to be a pastoral council, the watchword of which was *aggiornamento*.

John's optimism was widely shared before and during the council. There was unusual excitement among Catholics, especially in the so-called First World, and great expectations of changes on the way. Not doctrinal changes, but changes in the manner and practices of the Church. This optimism became ever more heady, fueled by the contemporaneous reports of the council sessions. An American priest in Rome who styled himself Xavier Rynne reported on the council for the *New Yorker*, reports which became published volumes, extending their influence. Secular journalists descended on Rome and a sort of para-council began, in which members of the media sought to exercise influence on the fathers of the council. Robert Blair Kaiser's early book, *Pope, Council, and World*, and even more his recent one, *Clerical Error: A True Story*, make it abundantly clear that a revolution was envisaged. At soirees sponsored by *Time* magazine, strategy and tactics were exuberantly discussed. And major pressure was to be put on changing the Church's attitude toward sexual morality.

It is worthwhile to recall for more than merely calendar reasons that the council took place during the decade called the '60s. These were the days of the sexual revolution, which consisted in separating the procreative from the unitive aspect of the sexual act. The estrogen pill and later developments provided chemical means of preventing birth, thus freeing the sexual act from the consequence of pregnancy. At first, at least within the Church, this was taken to have significance only for the married. Spouses seldom have as many children as they physically could or could reasonably afford, and thus, one way or another, they act to limit the number of their offspring. There were ways of doing this recognized as morally legitimate for Catholics, the most drastic being abstinence, another being the rhythm method, soon to be denigrated as Vatican Roulette. By this method, the wife took note of her fertile periods and, before engaging in the marital act, calculated at what point on her menstrual cycle she was; if naturally infertile, the spouses acted accordingly. The pill was seen as simplifying the matter. It rendered the woman incapable of conceiving throughout the month, and thus she could engage in the marital act at will. This, it was argued, was a tremendous boon to the married, and it was foreseen that happier and more harmonious marriages would result.

Of course, in the wider world, freedom from the consequence of pregnancy was seen as in itself a boon to women generally. Once only the male could flit from flower to flower with impunity; now the female was in a condition to behave as males presumably do. It is pregnancy and children that form the basis for any argument for permanence in marriage, since the couple must take on the task of nurturing, raising, and educating the children that result from their union. Now, thanks to the pill, there was a secure means of separating sexual activity and pregnancy. Indeed, the connection between the two came to seem wholly contingent. There was no longer any need to confine sexual activity to the married. Sexual liberation was the hallmark of the '60s.

Given the talk about opening windows to the world, such developments could scarcely be ignored when the bishops came to Rome, filed into St. Peter's, and took their places in council. However, early on, Pope John removed the issue of the pill from conciliar deliberations and appointed a committee to advise him on the matter. Of course, one finds in *Gaudium et Spes*, the conciliar document known as the Pastoral Constitution on the Church in the Modern World, a moving discussion on the sacrament of marriage and the reiteration of longtime and recent Church teaching on the matter. But the pill was not mentioned. For that matter, neither was that great enemy of the faith, the Soviet Union. The task of the committee appointed by John was to determine whether or not use of the pill fell under the Church's ban on artificial contraception. For many Catholics, the very fact that the pill was under discussion was a matter for high expectation. Of the two possible outcomes of the committee's deliberations, approval or disapproval, approval seemed to many to stand as good a chance as disapproval, if not better.

So matters stood when the first session ended. No documents had yet been produced. Pope John XXIII died and Paul VI, who was elected to succeed him, had the option of calling off the council or continuing it. He was eager that it go on. As for the birth control committee, he expanded its membership, and many of the new members were sympathetic to the acceptance of the pill. In the event, the committee was to expand its original mandate—to decide whether use of the pill was or was not an instance of artificial contraception—and called into question the very distinction between natural and artificial means of limiting births. Of course, within the Church, all this was still considered in the context of the sexual activity of married partners. A missionary bishop to India,

Thomas D. Roberts, published a book called *Contraception and Holiness*. The deliberations of the committee did not remain confidential, and soon it was rumored that the traditional ban on artificial contraception was to be lifted as having no logical basis. Eventually, the *National Catholic Reporter* (one of the organs most insistent that a new day was dawning and that much long taken as essential to Catholic doctrine was to be jettisoned) published a leaked document revealing that a majority of the committee was in favor of lifting the ban. The small minority opposed were portrayed as themselves unimpressed by the traditional arguments which they nonetheless advanced.

The council ended in 1965, as noted. The committee was an advisory committee, and the pope might or might not follow its advice. However, the notion spread like wildfire through the Church in Europe and North America that on matters sexual, the Church was joining the modern world. Seminarians were taught to expect the change, confessors anticipated it in dealing with penitents, and marriage preparation instructions assured those about to wed that they need not bother about artificial contraception, that is, they might licitly use the pill. This mood and these assumptions became increasingly commonplace. But years passed and Paul VI did not speak. Not to worry. How could he ignore the advice of the majority of the committee he himself had renewed and expanded? Finally, in July of 1968, Paul VI published the encyclical called *Humanae Vitae*. In it, he summarized Church teaching on marriage and went on to say that the unitive and procreative meanings of the marital act were inseparable. In short, he had refused the advice of the committee. The ban on artificial contraception, which of course was aimed at separating the two meanings of the act, stood.

This came as a bombshell to those who had convinced themselves that the ban on contraception was a dead letter. The reaction was unique in the history of the Catholic Church. Moral theologians took out a full-page ad in the *New York Times*, rejecting the decision of the pope and advising the faithful that they were not bound by it. The rebellion of the theologians had begun. It was to characterize and disrupt the life of the Church for decades, and is only now beginning to subside. In 1968 even some bishops' conferences seemed to waver, and there were individual bishops who openly rejected the encyclical. An auxiliary of the archdiocese of St. Paul, my old teacher and mentor James P. Shannon, abandoned his post and married, explaining his decision as due to his inability to embrace *Hu-*

manae Vitae or counsel the laity to abide by it. Some monsignors who owed their status to the pope tore off the piping from their cassocks, averring that they could not continue to show allegiance to Paul VI. Soon, it became customary to distinguish between the "official" teaching of the Church on sexual matters and the more liberal teaching that the faithful were advised to follow. What was clearly dissent from unequivocal Church teaching—the council itself had made clear the binding nature of encyclicals such as *Humanae Vitae*—became a kind of tradition among moral theologians. Many saw this as schism on its way.

■ It may seem odd to discuss the council in terms of sex, but no one who lived through these years will think so. Recently, the letters of an infatuated Karl Rahner, written to a woman while the Jesuit was deep in the affairs of the council, have been published. And Robert Blair Kaiser's wife was seduced by an Irish priest, Mallachy Martin, during those heady days. Hanky-panky is always with us, of course, but it is not always accompanied by self-serving rationales. Pope John Paul II, whose long reign, the third longest in the history of the papacy, extended into the third millennium, made the implementation of Vatican II the central aim of that reign. His emphasis was on those sixteen documents, drawn up, debated, and voted on by the fathers of the council and promulgated by Paul VI. Theological discussion of those documents went on, reasonably enough, and clarifying statements were issued from the Vatican. Strictly speaking, Vatican II *is* those documents, and any account of it ought ideally concentrate on them. But the tradition of dissent among Catholic theologians made that all but impossible.

Even during the council, reformers were invoking theological dissent on behalf of a mixed menu of matters. After 1968, theologians identified themselves as the second magisterium, the pope and bishops being the first. There was now rivalry between the two groups. Once the response to this would have been clear. One who rejected what the pope and his bishops taught would have seen himself, and been seen by others, to be rejecting the Church. The Protestant reformers might still consider themselves Christians, but they were clear that they were no longer Roman Catholics. But post-conciliar dissenters considered themselves to be, if not more Catholic than the pope, then certainly as Catholic. They saw themselves as ombudsmen intervening between the laity and an authoritarian and mistaken magisterium. They had no intention of leaving the Church. Their ambition was to have the Church conform to their views, however out of step with those of the first magisterium. Karl Rahner, who invented the notion of the second magisterium of theologians, noted that it was in contradiction with the first magisterium. What was the solution? Rahner said that time would decide. On the assumption that sexual morality is a serious matter, this seemed almost cynical. It certainly would not be much help to bewildered spouses who were receiving conflicting advice. Of course, most dissenting theologians thought the conflict chimerical. They were right, the pope was wrong, and people could take their word for it.

A full-blown crisis of teaching authority had emerged. In moral theology, the attack on traditional sexual morality was widened. What about masturbation, what about premarital and extramarital sex, what about homosexuality? A volume produced under the auspices of the Catholic Theological Society of America, *Human Sexuality*, called into question the traditional view on all these matters. Its discussion of homosexuality began by asking why we are so fearful of it, turning attention from what was ostensibly under discussion to what were clearly seen as benighted reactions to it. But the confrontational attitude toward traditional doctrine soon evolved into a questioning of the teaching authority of the pope and bishops as such. Such theologians appealed to the council against the pope, and soon were accusing John Paul II of trying to turn back the clock and overturn the changes introduced by Vatican II.

The controversy was by no means confined to the academy. Theologians became practiced in using the secular media to further their views. Men in Roman collars sat before television cameras and talked of the pope in ways that would have shamed the editor of *The Watchtower*. There was something addictive about such publicity, and to ensure more of it, the tendency was to become ever more outrageous. It is a good question whether theological dissent had its origin first in seminaries or in universities, but soon it characterized both. Men were ordained to the priesthood who had been taught by theological dissenters. Graduates of university programs in theology were finding employment in the bureaucracies which sprang up in dioceses and parishes. Sometimes it seemed as if all the faithful were likely to hear were views at variance with the magisterium.

■ Theologians like to describe themselves as ever under imminent threat of being silenced. During these years I almost longed to hear what a silent theologian would sound like. The events I have sketched with some semblance of objectivity were not matters of mere observation for me, nor could they have been for anyone calling himself a Catholic. From the earliest accounts of the council, there had been talk of liberals and conservatives, of left and right. Since a conservative Catholic was defined as one who accepted the magisterium of the Church, I became willy-nilly a conservative Catholic.

When I first heard of *Humanae Vitae,* I was mowing the yard, something in itself conducive to meditation, particularly when one is on a tractor mower. My first reaction was as a novelist, and I thought, Good Lord, this is my material. But in the days that followed, as I read the newspaper accounts of the papal encyclical and the increasingly comic reactions to it, I proposed to my agent a book to be called "How Many Children Has the Pope?" My thought was to oppose the media blitz of opposition to the encyclical with the reaction of a, well, conservative Catholic. I wrote some sample chapters and sent it to my agent. Nothing came of it. The zeitgeist was against me, of course, but maybe it wasn't that attractive a project. No matter. I had begun to think of a novel. The result was *The Priest,* of which I have already written.

One of the innovations of the council was the series of synods that met in Rome to discuss various issues. There were also extraordinary synods, the second of which was convened in 1985. I went to Rome as correspondent for *Crisis,* a magazine that Michael Novak and I had founded a few years earlier. Correspondents were not admitted to the sessions, but there were regular briefings in the Sala di Prenza. It was there that I became reacquainted with Richard John Neuhaus, whom I had first met at a Hartford meeting he had convened along with Peter Berger some years before. We issued a statement then, the Hartford Statement, the point of which was that Christianity does not entail any particular political view, that is, partisan view, whether of left or right. Richard was still a Lutheran then and also when we met again in Rome, but Richard and I were kindred spirits. Also visible and audible at these briefings was Peter Hebblethwaite, a laicized priest who functioned as Rome correspondent for *The Tablet* while usually remaining in England. But the extraordinary synod had brought him to his ostensible base. He was a Major Hooplish figure, fat and rumpled and sporting a vivid pair of suspenders. To say that Hebblethwaite had a chip on his sloping shoulders would be British in its understatement. Whenever he rose to speak, the voice of a dissenting Torquemada was heard in the hall. He was aggrieved by the proceedings and understandably so.

The Second Extraordinary Synod had been called to commemorate the twentieth anniversary of the close of Vatican II. For twenty years, the dissenters had operated with little objection or opposition, despite their claim that they faced imminent incarceration in the Castel San Angelo. Documents had indeed been issued in Rome that were mildly critical of them; indeed, from the point of view of magisterial teaching, it could be said that during these tumultuous years the clarity of Catholic doctrine reached an unprecedented peak, but what was lacking was practical implementation, let alone silencing of those who were sowing confusion in the Church. The Second Extraordinary Synod was the first official acknowledgment that there was something approaching schism in the Church. The final *reportatio* distinguished between a true and a false spirit of Vatican II, thus addressing the dissenters' claim that they represented the council in opposition to the papal magisterium. These two spirits were illustrated by lists of opposing claims. But alas, nothing was done to quell the false spirit of Vatican II. I returned home to find that the synod had little or no impact on life in the Catholic Church in America.

We were fighting the good fight in *Crisis,* and there were many other new publications, of course considered conservative, that came to the defense of the magisterium. The Fellowship of Catholic Scholars, under the leadership of the redoubtable Monsignor George Kelly, whose *The Battle for the American Church* is still one of the best books on what was going on, rallied academics to the support of the pope and bishops. The story of the Fellowship is symptomatic of those post-conciliar years. It was Kelly's thesis that the American bishops were seldom heard in defense of the magisterium because they had been cowed by the belief that Catholic intellectuals were in opposition to it. Kelly believed that once the bishops found that there was a vast cadre of professors and scholars who were faithful to the magisterium, episcopal spines would be strengthened and the successors of the Apostles would begin to sound as if they were. Kelly relinquished this belief only reluctantly and then only after years of holding it. When the bishops invited scholars to speak to them at their meetings, those invited were almost invariably dissenters. The test case was the 1990 document *Ex Corde Ecclesiae,* which dealt with the nature of the Catholic university. Here, Kelly believed, was something the bishops could rally round and oppose the drift of Catholic institutions of higher education into secularism. The draft guidelines for the implementation of *Ex Corde Ecclesiae* which the bishops drew up in 1993 immediately drew fire from dissenters, whereupon the bishops sat down with their critics to revise the guidelines.

Kelly had been secretary to Cardinal Spellman and had learned from that feisty prelate what it was like to be a bishop. He assumed that all bishops were potential Spellmans and only needed the necessary prompting to show it. Alas, it became clear that the hearts of all too many of the bishops were with the dissenters. The few who thought with the pope were worthy recipients of the Fellowship's Nicodemus award, Nicodemus having come to Jesus only under cover of darkness. Kelly eventually abandoned his theory and recognized that the bishops as a body were part of the problem, not of the solution.

At the Second Extraordinary Synod, Cardinal Bernard Law had proposed, in the interests of clarifying Catholic doctrine, that a new catechism be written, the catechism of Vatican II. This idea was enthusiastically received, and eventually the future Cardinal Christoph Schoenbrun, then a simple but wise Dominican friar, was made editor of the project. Eventually the catechism was done, first in French, eventually of course in Latin. Then arose the question of the English translation. The American bishops, who had been tolerant of the International Commission on English in the Liturgy (ICEL), the group that had turned the liturgy in English-speaking countries into a kind of Esperanto, commissioned a draft translation that, in the eyes of members of the Fellowship of Catholic Scholars, notably Monsignor Michael Wrenn and Ken Whitehead, blurred and even altered the text. The Fellowship went into battle, with the result that the published English translation was faithful to the original.

It was the need for such battles that characterized the post-conciliar Church. The bishops seemed chiefly concerned to placate dissenters and the secular media and countenanced an initial translation that would have deprived the faithful of one of the most precious results of the council. Far more serious, although its consequences ticked away like a time bomb for years, was the demoralization, in every sense of the term, of a depressing number of priests.

The early days of the council saw the mass exodus into the laicized state, with or without official permission, of a significant percentage of the priests of the United States. Nuns, who had once outnumbered priests and who had a long and noble history in the schools and hospitals, seemed to go berserk. Feminism of the most secular sort captured many, and the devastating psychological ministrations of Carl Rogers and others infected many communities with the sexual liberation of the time. The habit went swiftly, first modified into forms that seemed the revenge of couturiers, then abandoned entirely. The number of nuns dropped precipitously. There was little surprise in this. How could orders that seemed intent on bemoaning the slings and arrows that they had suffered from a paternalistic Church attract new recruits? As for the priests, it is difficult not to see a relationship between the sexual activity of supposed celibates, which eventually became notorious, and the confusion in moral theology wrought by the dissenters.

Against this view can be urged the undoubted fact that many of the priests who are currently costing the Church millions upon millions of dollars in court-ordered payments were already priests before the collapse of moral theology. Their training surely would have enabled them to see that adulterous and homosexual activities were morally wrong. How can one explain this? I will provide an anecdote.

Priests of that age, though not only they, were regularly sent to programs allegedly designed to familiarize them with the brave new postconciliar world. There was such a program at Notre Dame. A St. Paul priest I had known years before, who had been engaged in dedicated and effective pastoral work, came to Notre Dame to be renewed. We had lunch one day in the University Club. After pleasant reminiscing, it became clear that he wanted to talk about what he was undergoing. He leaned across the table and said to me in a whisper, "They told us to forget everything we had been taught in the seminary." Perhaps the one speaking to those priests was indulging in hyperbole, a little rhetorical excess to gain attention. Perhaps. The effect on my old friend was obvious. He was not, I can say, a fast-ball pitcher in the seminary, but he was a good priest. He had walked in the vocation to which he had been called. Now he was being told to forget everything that had defined his life. How could he not feel vertigo? He finished the course and went home and a few years later left the priesthood, under a cloud of accusations of sexual irregularity.

Clearly not only the young and uninformed were affected by the confusion in moral theology. One of the more bizarre accusations of dissenters was that the Church was obsessed with sex. But it became inescapable that at the root of dissent, at the bottom of the dismissal of doctrinal authority, was an obsession with sex, most particularly with the continuing justification of the repudiation of *Humanae Vitae.* I have written of this in a little book called *What Went Wrong with Vatican II?* There you will find an analysis of a 1990 report from a committee of the Catholic Theological Society of America, which deals with the canonical requirement that those who teach Catholic theology do so as lieutenants of the teaching Church and thus must have a mandate from the bishop to teach. No one familiar with the track record of theologians would have expected this report to explain and defend this requirement. *Au contraire.* First, the report cast doubt on whether such a requirement could be made of those teaching in universities. But the heart of the matter was reached when it addressed the two elements required to receive a mandate. Those requirements are the recitation of the Nicene Creed and the avowal that one accepts the teachings of the Catholic Church. The uninformed onlooker might well wonder why any Catholic theologian would bridle at these. One found the reason in a footnote. It might be thought, according to the report, that one who said he accepted the teachings of the Church was thereby accepting *Humanae Vitae.* So there it was. All these years later, we were still in 1968.

■   Vatican II was the most important event in Catholicism in the twentieth century. It would be nice if one could think of it only in terms of the sixteen conciliar documents promulgated by Paul VI. Some are admittedly controversial, but all are wonderful, and for a Catholic they are measures of his faith. Pope John's original intention that the council was called, not to define doctrine, but to seek ways of making it more effective in the modern world, was not fulfilled. Some of the documents are dogmatic, and those who seek to downplay the council as simply concerned with contingent judgments of a pastoral sort, not binding on the faithful, seem to me clearly wrong. For all that, it is not those documents which leap to mind when one hears references to the council.

For one thing, the documents, like the many encyclicals of John Paul II, have not had the desired impact. It is easy to share John Paul's view that the full effect of the council has yet to be felt. What has been felt, daily and insistently, is what in 1985 was called the false spirit of Vatican II. The council has been invoked to justify doctrines and practices clearly at variance with it and the whole tradition of the Church. When this is observed, one is called a fundamentalist, enamored of the letter and not the spirit of the council. Of course the question is which spirit is being referred to.

We have come a long way since December 8, 1965, when the council closed. Already, perceptive Catholics, like Jacques Maritain in his *The Peasant of the Garonne,* were warning against what Maritain called kneeling to the world. No one at the time could have foreseen the turmoil and confusion that lay ahead: a liturgy made banal, homilies which tried the patience of congregations, blithe dismissals of clear teaching. There emerged a generation of Catholics all but illiterate in the faith they professed. Worse, the faith became what one chose to make it. One of the greatest scandals in the United States has been the number of elected officials, representatives and senators, who have not simply acquiesced in programs at variance with their professed faith, but have become their spokesmen and champions. Their mantra was provided by Governor Mario Cuomo of New York, who said that while he was personally opposed to abortion, he could not impose his views on his fellow citizens. The difficulty was that he allowed some of his fellow citizens to dictate what he could publicly hold. It could be said that our bishops stood firm on opposing abortion, if nothing else, but until quite recently they have not reproached Catholic politicians who were champions of abortion. Then a bishop in California warned the then governor that he could not receive communion, and later the then bishop of Lacrosse, Wisconsin, wrote a letter to Catholic politicians of the sort described and warned them that their position was untenable. A few other bishops spoke. The response of the politicians was that they could not be dictated to in their public role by the Church. Of course it is not a matter of telling a politician how to vote; it is a matter of reminding Catholic politicians that certain policies they espouse are opposed both to common morality and to the explicit teachings of their Church. Surely, if a politician's choice was to vote for or against an immoral policy, such as abortion, his Catholic conscience should tell him that if resignation is the only choice, then he should resign.

By their long silence the bishops in effect acquiesced in the privatization of religious beliefs, and not only religious beliefs; moral principles of a sort unacceptable to the media and to various pressure groups were declared out of place in the public forum. John Courtney Murray, a Jesuit whose writings were said to have influenced the Vatican II declaration on religious liberty, had held that what made America work was the fact that, beneath and presupposed by the religious beliefs that separate us, was a common morality that sustained our public life. Now we seem to have arrived at a time when, in the minds of many judges and legal scholars, morality is as irrelevant as religious belief in our public life. Whether any nation or community can survive on that assumption is the great question. Doubtless, we are partially saved by the inconsistency of judicial decisions, but for how long will that be the case?

■ Catholics my age were brought up in a Church whose doctrine and practices were clear. There were few quibbles with doctrine, but of course, humans being what we are, conduct was not always in tune with professed belief. But the adulterer knew that adultery was a sin and hoped for the grace to confess and receive pardon and peace. Not everyone waited for the wedding ceremony to enjoy the delights of love, but there was no tendency to maintain that fornication was now all right. Many have spoken of the loss of the sense of sin in the post-conciliar Church, and doubtless this is what they mean.

Have I become a Cassandra, in despair of the Church and the modern world? Not at all. With William Faulkner in his Nobel Prize address, I am confident that man will prevail, and as for the Church, the gates of hell will not prevail against her. But one would have to be a mindless Pollyanna not to admit that we live in strange and antinomian times. Still, all such judgments are historical. Kierkegaard accused Hegel of fusing, as in the preface to *The Philosophy of History*, the historical and ethical appraisals of action. But the historical, in Kierkegaard's phrase, obeys a quantitative dialectic, whereas the moral realm is the qualitative. The vast majority of human beings would be insignificant ciphers if their importance were taken to be historical. Most of us will not figure in even a footnote of the history of our times. If the historical estimate, apart from being chancy in itself, is governed by the extrinsic, our historical judgments can never reach to those wellsprings of action—reason and will—thanks to which every person is of infinite value. We really never know what is going on, even under our very noses.

Nonetheless, responding to the council, one seeks to read the signs of the time. All around me I see signs that we are at last emerging from the post-conciliar chaos. Recent episcopal appointments encourage the view that the future will not be like the past. A new generation of priests has become a source of anguish to Andrew Greeley and Richard McBrien, put off by what they see as a docile orthodoxy. New orders and seminaries are producing such priests, and even older seminaries, once a source of scandal, are slowly regaining their *raison d'être*. Perhaps John Paul II has brought the bark of Peter through choppy seas and the true spirit of Vatican II can begin to have its full effect.

I should say that I have never doubted the sincerity of those I have called dissenting theologians. Many of them are friends of mine. Richard McBrien, whom I just mentioned, is a charming, personable man. I am unlikely to forget that during my wife's last illness, he wrote her a lovely letter in which he told her he would offer a Mass for her recovery. After her death, he wrote an equally moving letter to me. It could have come from the most thoughtful pre-conciliar Irish pastor. Perhaps it was the fact that, beneath the differences and debates of these parlous times, the interlocutors shared the same faith that made the experience tolerable all around.

From time to time, I think of all the priests who left the priesthood and are now, most of them, as old as I am, perhaps older. What thoughts must come as the shadows lengthen? Recently, at Mass in Kilkenny Cathedral, I was forcibly struck by this thought, and I stayed behind remembering name after name, hoping that all goes well with them and that they and all of us who have been to some degree casualties of Vatican II will soon meet merrily in heaven.

EDITOR AND PUBLISHER

WE SHOULD BE CAREFUL OF THE GIFTS WE GIVE CHILDREN. WHEN I was seven or eight I got as a Christmas present a printing set. A box of rubber letters, a wooden bar to set them in, a stamp pad. It had to be inexpensive, this was during the Depression, but it filled me with excitement, and I set to work. Inking letters and impressing them on paper may not seem the most exciting or creative of activities, but I reveled in it. Of course, the question then arose as to what to print. Sometime later there was a sort of typewriter, a gift common to me and my brothers, I think. There was a wheel in the center with letters around its rim, and one composed by turning the wheel to the desired letter and pressing down. A turn of the wheel, another punch, soon words appeared on paper. It was made of metal, tinny, one step up from the punch-out metal cars one found in boxes of Cracker Jacks that were labeled "Made in Japan," a phrase then synonymous with cheap and junky. With that typewriter, I produced the first issue of the 27th Avenue Paper, illustrated by my brothers, Ray and Rog. Of course there was only the one issue, but that initiation into the physical activity of putting words on paper with an eye to possible readers imprinted itself on my psyche. More of the same would follow.

At Nazareth Hall, as I have mentioned, my first involvement with the school magazine, the *Puer Nazarenus,* was on the production end, helping John Murphy mimeograph the issues. Ah, the distinctive smell of the ink used in those great-barreled machines invented by Thomas Edison, the stained fingers, the satisfaction when a sufficient number of copies of a page had been made and one changed the stencil and began another. When all the pages were done and dry, we stapled them together, and the new issue was ready for distribution. When I became editor, the process was changed and the magazine was offprinted, but that entailed getting copy ready for the printer. Much earlier, after my second year at Nazareth Hall, I landed a summer job at Syndicate Printing in downtown Minneapolis, kitty-corner from what was then just the *Minneapolis Star Journal* (the *Star* eventually gobbled up the third local newspaper, as it had the second, and became for a time the *Star Journal Tribune*). I got the job because Gerry O'Neill, a grade-school classmate, was working there courtesy of his mother, who knew the owner. Our task was to deliver proofs to customers, on foot, carrying them through downtown streets to various businesses. Between deliveries we could watch the men operating the linotype machines, setting type by hand, running the presses. It was the job press that fascinated me. You set a galley, inked it, then brought a roller over it, and the image appeared on paper; it was all done by human power. My job paid the then minimum wage of forty cents an hour, so I was making twenty dollars a week, a step up from caddying at the Minnikada Club. On Saturdays, Gerry and I worked mornings in the empty shop, cleaning up. We did this as quickly as possible and then spent the rest of the morning working the job press. I made note paper headed by "From the Desk of Ralph McInerny." I printed cards. I made book plates. Some days we would just set a number of engraved illustrations and run them off to see how they looked. The ink used on the job press came in cylindrical cartons and had an aroma that was intoxicating. No wonder I felt an affinity with those printer's devils, Mark Twain and William Dean Howells.

It became known that I was a seminarian. I began to get teased by printers who seemed to wonder if I knew about girls. The whole notion of celibacy was remote to me at the time—most boys of fifteen are celibates perforce, so the prospect is hardly menacing. A woman who worked in shipping, Shirley, was enlisted to put me to the kind of test Thomas Aquinas's brothers must have devised to try his vocation. I suppose she was in her late twenties, pretty, plump, and concupiscible. One afternoon I was lifted onto a shipping table and held down by a couple of printers while Shirley planted supposedly seductive kisses on my virginal lips. Of course that was all. My reaction was not exactly Thomistic, I found it all oddly flattering, but I was never quite at ease with Shirley afterward.

A little neighborhood paper, editorship of the school magazine, an introduction to printing, where would it all lead? Later, while I was doing graduate work at the University of Minnesota and working at the Catholic Youth Center in Minneapolis part time, I edited a little paper called *Contact,* aimed at teenagers. I wrote most of it myself, and when I wasn't doing that I wrote poems to Connie on postcards and mailed them off. I found them among her things after she died. My editorial life went into idle until 1965, when John Oesterle was named editor of *The New Scholasticism,* the journal of the American Catholic Philosophical Association. I was named his associate editor and while he lived, we put out that hallowed quarterly together. When John died in 1977, I was named editor and with his widow, Jean, continued to edit *The New Scholasticism* until 1988. Much later I was on the staff of *The Center Journal,* founded by an old student of mine, Kerry Kohler, but my next serious work as an editor began when Michael Novak and I had a fateful conversation in 1982.

Michael was already a very productive writer. (In his novel *The Tiber Was Silver* there is a minor character named McInerny, but we did not know one another at the time.) Over the years, Michael and I had written articles for *Commonweal* and *America,* but we came to find ourselves out of sympathy with the editorial line they were taking after the Vatican II Council. *Commonweal* had always had the reputation of a liberal publication, in the best sense of the word. The rector of St. Paul Seminary, Monsignor Rudoph Bandas, despised *Commonweal,* and there was a joke about the seminarian who included among his sins to a visiting confessor that he had read *Commonweal.* The astonished priest assured him that that was not a sin. "But, Father," he whispered. " I took pleasure in it." Well, Mike and I had ceased taking pleasure in reading either *Commonweal* or *America.* Mike was well along on his rightward swing and I was where I have always been. We began to talk of the possibility of a magazine, and *Crisis* was born.

At first we called it *Catholicism in Crisis,* an obvious rip-off, but soon shortened it to *Crisis.* We were then contacted by lawyers for the NAACP, whose journal was also called *Crisis.* There were edgy communications back and forth, but finally they forgot their objections. It would be difficult to think of the two magazines as competing for the same readers. Michael was in Washington, D.C., at the American Enterprise Institute, and I of course was at Notre Dame, but such a separation no longer presented the difficulties it would have before the electronic innovations that were to revolutionize publishing. Indeed, with the advent of the personal computer and publishing programs it became too easy to launch at least a newsletter, most of them appallingly bad. I agreed to serve as editor and set to work. Of course Mike and I were in constant communication, but when the first issue appeared he was nonetheless surprised. He had thought we were going to put out a newsletter. From the beginning my own ambition, not to put too fine a point on it, was to engage *America* and *Commonweal* frontally. In Milford, Indiana, was a printing establishment with a web press that could produce publications on newsprint. Alice Osberger, my secretary since 1979, eventually elevated to the title of Administrative Assistant, unflappingly added to her many roles that of editorial assistant. The first issue of *Crisis* was not many notches above my old neighborhood paper, but it looked vaguely like its putative rivals, and we were on our way.

Mike was still in the grips of the idea that opponents on the matters that interested us could somehow come together; all it would take was conversation and working together. Accordingly, he wanted our editorial board to include liberals as well as conservatives. Ed Marciniak, of Chicago, no one's idea of a conservative, was on the board for several years. Mike thought that he had got John Noonan's agreement to serve on the board, and when the first issue appeared, Noonan was listed as a board member. He was flabbergasted. He telephoned. He denied ever having given his permission. He explained that he had to be careful how his name was used! Of course we took him off the board. He is now a federal judge on the circuit court in California. If he had stayed with us he might now be a justice of the Supreme Court.

Noonan's reaction was *sui generis.* Others were furious at the line *Crisis* was taking. Colleagues wrote letters to Father Hesburgh, demanding that he shut me down. The idea of something other than the usual liberal gruel coming out of Notre Dame, and associated with the Jacques Maritain Center! (I was then director of both the Center and the university's Medieval Institute.) Father Hesburgh passed them all on to me, providing me with one of the surprises of my life. I suppose that until then I thought all my colleagues more or less liked me; there had never been any reason to think otherwise. Now, reading the venomous condemnations of *Crisis*, and myself, was a revelation. I was particularly stung by the charge that I was diverting university money to this project. Mike and I had announced the formation of our magazine in Washington in a press conference held at the AFL-CIO headquarters. The first question was: who is bankrolling this? The suggestion was that some sinister Daddy Warbucks had bought our souls and we were dancing to his tune. Someone, I can only guess who, prevailed upon old friends of Jacques Maritain to write me, and I received a plaintive note from Olivier Lecombe, now Cardinal Lecombe, who seemed unsure what it was he was supposed to object to. Of course Father Hesburgh did not do what he was asked to. Unlike the objectors, he was genuinely liberal, tolerant of viewpoints he did not share, sometimes I thought too tolerant, but surely in this case as right as rain.

I rented office space in downtown South Bend, where first Terry Hall and then Phil Lawler worked for the magazine. In the afternoon I would stop by. The offices were in the remodeled Lasalle Hotel, in whose bar Frank O'Malley had spent many hours. Now it was an office building. Bruce Fingerhut also had offices there. The initial reaction by those letter writers provided me with an important lesson. Never be vulnerable in the matter of money. People who cannot refute what you say will hope to accuse you of peculation. Alice became a bookkeeper, too, and thanks to her I can account to the penny for whatever money I receive and dispense. I never took a salary from *Crisis,* indeed, have never earned a nickel from the magazine. Mike and I began by contributing a thousand dollars apiece, money well invested, but the reward is the magazine, which continues to thrive.

Once the magazine was established and I had done my stint as editor, Mike took his turn and we rented offices in Washington. Scott Walter and Dinesh D'Souza at first helped Mike, and then themselves became editors. In South Bend I also launched Crisis Books, and we published a number of volumes.

A magazine makes demands on one's time. No sooner is one issue off to the printer then the next one has to be prepared. And the next and the next. Eventually, Mike and I felt that we had accomplished what we set out to do, and were ready to turn *Crisis* over to a new generation. Accordingly, in 1994, after a few overtures on the telephone, I met with Deal Hudson in Aspen, Colorado, where we were taking part in a tribute to

Mortimer Adler. We sat in the sun and sipped beer, and I arranged the transfer of the magazine to him. He was to receive it as a gift, lock, stock and barrel. There was some money to turn over, but basically we were giving him the right to raise money to sustain the magazine as well as edit it. As far as I knew, Deal was still a tenured professor of philosophy at Fordham. Taking on *Crisis* thus presumably represented a huge gamble for him. The plan was a trial year, and then permanency if we were all satisfied. In the event, we made it permanent long before the year was up. Under Deal, *Crisis* altered, of course, bearing his stamp, as it should have. Until recently I continued to write for *Crisis*—for twenty years and more there was never an issue in which I did not appear—for the fun of it, but also to exhibit my continuing support.

■   Like Trollope's warden, I now began to play an imaginary cello; like the prisoner in Dickens, I missed my last. But not for long. Father Fessio, the founder of Ignatius Press, the Sheed & Ward of post-conciliar Catholicism, was providing a home for a number of magazines, new and old, which profited from the publicity Ignatius could offer. We began talking because he thought I still controlled *Crisis*, but soon we were talking of a new magazine. Father Fessio would provide the services of Ignatius Press for printing and distribution; all I would have to do is the editorial work. And so *Catholic Dossier* was born. I had suggested calling it *McCatholic* and the counter suggestion was *Confessio*—never try to be wittier than a Jesuit—so we called it *Catholic Dossier*. It appeared every two months, six times a year, and unlike *Crisis* it was to be thematic. My thought was that what many had lost was the wider Catholic culture that sustains the Church's teaching on contraception, abortion, and all those doctrines which had become so controversial. Divorced from the wider setting, or worse, simply inserted into the dominant secular viewpoint, they could seem quirky and odd even to the faithful. So *Catholic Dossier* would take up such issues and place them in the Catholic context where they alone made sense.

Father Fessio had a business plan drawn up, according to which, after some years, we were to reach a level of subscribers that spelled success. We reached it during the first year. The goal was modest enough, but still it was heady to get such a reception. It was Father Fessio's idea that I should include in every issue a Father Dowling short story. Supposedly this would capture the interest of my army of fans. Whether or not it did help, I agreed, and in every issue there appeared a five-thousand-word Dowling story. The pastor of St. Hilary's in Fox River had previously performed only in novels, so this was a departure, and I came to love writing about him at that length. As often as not, the germ of my story would follow from thinking about the housekeeper Marie Murkin. Over the years, a considerable number of these short stories accumulated. Marty Greenburg, my entrepreneurial friend, has arranged for a collection of them to appear in book form. Marty works out of Green Bay, Wisconsin, and I had come to know him when he asked to reprint a story of mine that had appeared in *Ellery Queen Mystery Magazine*. Eventually, I edited several such anthologies for him. But Marty is another story.

Issues of *Catholic Dossier* were devoted to such topics as the Crusades, Edith Stein, the ministry of bishops, the Reformation, American saints, contraception, homosexuality, the liturgy, *Gaudium et Spes*, religious liberty, Pope Pius XII, Scripture, marriage, Catholicism in America, Catholic writers, the Catholic diaspora, and on and on. The magazine was more or less a seven-year itch. When we discontinued publication, there was a gratifying expression of dismay by readers, but I felt that we had done what we set out to do. And Father Fessio was being lured into the chancellorship of Ave Maria University. Since then, I sometimes find myself again playing that imaginary instrument and repairing invisible shoes, but I do not think I will launch another serial publication.

■ Bruce Fingerhut is a bear of a man, with more hair on his face than on his head, who entered the Church via Episcopalianism. He came to South Bend to study political philosophy with Gerhart Niemeyer, but he was too nice for the academic life. Like all the entrepreneurs I know, he is a dreamer, about as practical as your guardian angel. He and his wife, Laila, founded a school they called Magdalene but met with the formidable competition of Stanley Clark, another South Bend private school. Bruce then went to work for the Notre Dame Press, learned the trade, and talked Henry Regnery into a partnership in Gateway Editions, the paperback imprint of the firm Henry had sold to a son-in-law. They set up shop on the top floor of Tippecanoe Place, a former Studebaker mansion in downtown South Bend, and, besides important books, published my novel *Spinnaker*. It came out in 1977, just before we left for Rome, and there was a party on the first floor of the Tippencanoe mansion to launch the book. Bishop Sheridan, the episcopal bishop of Indiana, was there, a festive occasion. The success of Gateway brought younger Regnerys into the firm. And tragedy struck. A Regnery son, on his way to the American Book Association convention in San Francisco, was in a plane that crashed after taking off from O'Hare Airport. Things were never the same again. Blood is thicker than water, and Bruce was not a Regnery.

Bruce went on to found Icarus Press and soon had a list as long as your arm, but, like Icarus, he made a fatal mistake. In order to publish the kind of books he wanted to, he published others meant to finance the project. Alas, the meretricious tail began to wag the dog. And these were parlous times, economically speaking. Bruce fought the good fight, but the exorbitant interest charged on the money he borrowed made any profit impossible. Eventually, he threw in the towel. Then he recouped with a brilliant idea, *Books in Philosophy.* It was one of the best entrepreneurial ideas ever conceived. Bruce became a bookstore without a store, advertising through an increasingly larger tabloid catalogue—he had arrangements with just about every publisher of philosophical titles. He was a mail-order bookstore. If he had put it on the Internet, he would have anticipated Amazon.com. Even so, he had a tremendous success. Whereupon he sold the business to *Philosophers Index* and founded St. Augustine's Press, which was soon to rival Ignatius. This time, Bruce published only the books he really wanted to.

Bruce and I collaborated on a number of projects. The first was Cram Cassettes, which was a version of Cliffs Notes. I wrote summaries of dozens of great books, my son David recorded these summaries on cassettes, and Bruce marketed them, all done up in a plastic package. What I remember of those days are the flow charts Bruce produced, marvelously detailed plans that bore little relation to the actual history of the business. I lost a lot of money. I was not sorry to see the project sink. From medieval times, digests and outlines of texts have figured in university education, but I do not really approve of them. By that time we had a second idea.

Over the course of my teaching career, which has always involved the works of Thomas Aquinas, I had seen knowledge of Latin more or less disappear. At the beginning, when I gave a course on one of Thomas's commentaries on Aristotle, students could easily read the original. I vividly remember the first time I looked out and saw the terrified look on students' faces when I assigned readings. They needed translations. I began the habit of preparing double-column handouts of the texts I intended to use, with Latin on the left, English on the right. English translations of some of these commentaries had been published, but in the post-conciliar flight from Thomism, they had gone out of print. Copies of them could be found, but only at very high prices. Why not get the rights of those and reissue them? Bruce and I talked, and Dumb Ox Books was formed. If I ever make it into a footnote of the history of these times, I suspect it will be because of Dumb Ox Books. First we secured the rights to the commentaries on the *Nicomachean Ethics* and the *Metaphysics*. These had been published by Henry Regnery. I scanned the text onto disks and amended and added to them in a modest way, and Bruce put them into camera-ready copy and engaged a printer. And the books were publicized by St. Augustine's Press. Our idea was not to make a profit, but rather to use the money earned by rolling it over to finance the next title. This we have done, bringing out Thomas's commentaries on the *Physics* and *De anima*, as well as on the *Ethics* and *Metaphysics*. Those on the *Perihermeneias* and *Posterior Analytics* are in production. They come out both in hardback and paperback, the latter priced within the budgets of graduate students.

I serve on the board of St. Augustine's Press, and my admiration for what Bruce has done is profound. He has housed his publishing venture in various rented offices, but of late he operates out of his home. Despite the elegance of the volumes and the sophistication of sales and distribution, St. Augustine's Press is in many ways a cottage industry, with Laila and now Bruce's son trying to wrest some of the work away from Bruce. Bruce was also involved in another publishing project of mine.

■ When I succeeded Joe Evans as director of the Jacques Maritain Center, I was wise enough to know that I could never be another Joe Evans. This tall and mystic man had translated a number of Maritain's books, but his main effort went into teaching courses in Maritain and being totally available to students in the Center, which was located first in the old library, now Bond Hall, the architecture building, but in 1963 moved to the seventh floor of the new library along with the Medieval Institute. The Maritain Center and the Medieval Institute are adjacent to one another, and during the years when I directed both, I had a door opened between them. My academic life since 1963 has been spent in the library,

first in a basement office, then in the offices of *The New Scholasticism,*
which were originally located on the eleventh floor before being moved
down to the fifth and eventually back up to the seventh floor, under the
wing of the Maritain Center. Jean Oesterle was also ensconced on the seventh floor in an office Father Hesburgh arranged to be fashioned for her
from space occupied by a number of graduate student carrels. Here she
worked until her ninetieth year, translating the *Disputed Questions on Evil*
of Thomas Aquinas after our long work with *The New Scholasticism* ceased.

There was no job description for the director of the Maritain Center. I
decided to do two things. The first was to gather the papers of giants of
the Thomistic Revival besides the modest amount of Maritain material
we already had. Maritain had been present when the Center was founded
in 1957, and the original idea was that it would become the repository of
his papers. When Raïssa died and Jacques' life became centered at Tou-
louse and Kolbsheim, the plan changed and the bulk of his papers ended
up, fittingly enough, in Kolbsheim. Yves Simon, a student of Maritain's
who had taught first at Notre Dame and then at the University of Chicago, bequeathed to the Center his letters and the elements of the vast en-
cyclopedic philosophical work on which he was engaged. The Simon
papers are the jewel of our collection. From Laval I obtained copies of
the Charles De Koninck papers. Historical interest in Thomism and the
Thomistic Revival is quickening, as witness the little book of Romanus
Cessario (*A Short History of Thomism*) and others. In the post-conciliar
reaction against Thomas and scholasticism, accounts of what the past
had been like became parodies. Never trust a reformer's account of what
he intends to reform. Now that the dust has settled, including the dust
that was once the reformer, a more balanced estimate can be made of the
strengths and weaknesses of that period.

My second project was to bring out a twenty-volume set of Maritain
in English. From Kolbsheim was appearing what eventually became the
sixteen volumes of the *Oeuvres de Jacques et Raïssa Maritain,* under the
general direction of René Mougel. This was a far more scholarly project
than the one I intended, but of course it made my project considerably
easier. Not all of Maritain's works had been translated into English, and
some of the existing translations were inadequate. Having worked out
the plan of the twenty volumes, I then engaged certain people as editors
of the volumes. The editor's task was to assess the existing English translation, if there was one, and suggest either amending or replacing it. Most

volumes would include several works of Maritain. Bernard Doering, my colleague at Notre Dame, translated *Approches sans Entraves*. This had appeared after Maritain's death, and Doering's translation, *Untrammeled Approaches*, became the last of our projected twenty volumes, although it was the first to appear. Almost simultaneously, *The Degrees of Knowledge* appeared. Our publisher is the University of Notre Dame Press. Once under way, the idea was that at least one volume would appear each year. Alas, plans gang oft agley. A production glitch held up the projected volume 1, *The Bergsonian Philosophy*, for several years. John O'Callaghan, my colleague in the philosophy department and now director of the Maritain Center, has assumed responsibility for this project, and there should be smooth sailing ahead.

■ Jacques Maritain (1882–1973), a Frenchman, a layman, and a convert to Catholicism, became one of the most prominent figures in the Thomistic Revival. During World War II, the Maritains found themselves with other exiles in New York, and Raïssa wrote two volumes of memoirs, *We Have Been Friends Together* and *Adventures in Grace*, which were avidly read. They made American readers feel like members of the group of pre-war friends of the Maritains, most of whom had also attended the Thomistic seminars arranged annually at the Maritains' home in Meudon, outside Paris. Jacques was a philosopher with a difference. When he came into the Church from an atheistic period, and Raïssa too—she having abandoned the Judaism of her girlhood—their godfather was the tempestuous Léon Bloy, whose novel *The Woman Who Was Poor* contained the memorable line, "There is only one tragedy, not to be a saint." Under the aegis of Thomas Aquinas, the couple saw the intellectual and spiritual lives as complementary. Philosophers too should be in pursuit of holiness. There is no need to say how countercultural this was. As narrated by Raïssa, their lives inspired generations of artists, writers, musicians, poets, theologians, and philosophers. Theirs was an integral Thomism.

The first philosophical work I ever read, at Nazareth Hall, a gift from Father Gorman, was Maritain's *Introduction to Philosophy*. This was more fateful than I knew, but when I went on to the seminary I realized that philosophy and I were to have a lifelong love affair, and by philosophy I mean that of Thomas Aquinas. The Thomistic Revival saw the kind of thought represented by Thomas as a remedy for the cultural woes of the day. The title of Maritain's first book, *Antimoderne,* conveyed something of that spirit, although Maritain, like most Thomists, was not a medievalist looking backward, but a philosopher for whom the thought of Thomas was relevant for the times. He was not repudiating the time in which he lived; he was rejecting certain dominant assumptions about man and society. And he saw the cure and alternative as coming from the assimilation of the thought of St. Thomas.

No one can understand the Thomistic Revival without grasping the vocational understanding of philosophy. The Catholic who engages in philosophy is part of a tradition that stretches back through the centuries, and his task is to appropriate that patrimony and make it part of the contemporary conversation. But this is not a question of merely winning arguments. The pursuit of the truth is a personal matter, however objective the truth sought. It was the genius of Maritain always to keep before us that personal dimension of the philosophical task. Not many philosophers contemporary with him would have thought of themselves as in pursuit of holiness. Eventually, as a tribute to Maritain's influence on me and on many others, I wrote *The Very Rich Hours of Jacques Maritain: A Spiritual Life,* and I advise any reader captivated by this little sketch to turn to it.

■ Not everyone was enthralled by my direction of the Medieval Institute. I emphasized what I thought we could deliver to students: intellectual history with the focus on philosophy and theology and medieval universities. During my seven years as director, many students earned master's or doctoral degrees, and people who received their doctorates then are in colleges and universities across the land. A number of books were published under the institute's auspices, including my friend Marilyn McCord Adams's two-volume study of William Ockham and books by Mark Jordan and Stephen Gersh. An exhibition of original drawings from the Ambrosiana toured the country for over a year under the auspices of the Medieval Institute, and Randy Coleman produced a magnificent catalog of the collection. Distinguished lecturers came and spoke in the institute reading room. And seated on one side of the podium (I was on the other), facing the audience, was Canon Astrik Gabriel.

One of the first questions Father Hesburgh asked me when he appointed me director of the Medieval Institute was, "Can you get along with Gabriel?" I told him yes, I could get along with anybody. Well, Astrik Gabriel was not just anybody. He was the second director of the institute (recommended by Étienne Gilson), a native of Hungary, and, to put it mildly, a personality. In my early years at Notre Dame, the Medieval Institute was housed in the southwest corner on the second floor of the old library, and I would go there to make use of Migne's *Patrologia Latina*. This was before copying machines, and these were volumes either impossible to obtain as personal copies or prohibitively priced. I have often thought that my labors there were not unlike those of a medieval scholar. Much of the time I spent writing out texts for my own use. I might have been in a monastic scriptorium in the twelfth century. To work in the library of the Medieval Institute was perforce to be aware of the presence of the director, Astrik Gabriel. A portly Friar Tuck of a man, his hair already sparse and silver, with a large meaty face on which expressions seemed to be displayed like exhibits, his shouting passage through the rooms punctuated the otherwise placid silence of the place. The librarian then was Francis Lazenby, a learned man who had been turned into a trembling obsequious servant by the demanding director. "Dr. Lazenby!" would be shouted from the inner sanctum, and Lazenby would scramble to his feet and hurry to his master. In Gabriel, one might have thought, we had a martinet indeed.

In those days he drove, and there was a spot along the south wall of the library he took to be his. There was no official sanction for this, just custom. One day I parked my car in that spot. Gabriel arrived, found his spot taken, and flew into a rage. I could hear him coming up the stairs with a librarian or two in tow, shouting his indignation to the four winds. He stormed into the institute library. Of course he did not know whose car had violated his sense of turf. I went on working. In expressing his rage, Gabriel kept saying, "I am full professor, I am full professor." Full of what? I did not say aloud. When I left I went to my car circuitously, got in, and sped away. "Can you get along with Gabriel?" Father Hesburgh asked.

When I became director I received at the same time the Michael P. Grace Chair in Medieval Studies. My predecessor as director, Jeffrey Russell, had also held this chaired professorship before me. Gabriel, who had labored long and through the heat of the day, not only had not been made a chaired professor—there were in any case only a handful of them then—he had been forced to retire at the age of sixty-five. This was mandatory for all at the time, but Gabriel expected and did not get an exemption from this requirement. He brooded. He shook his leonine head until his dewlaps swayed, and there was fire in his eye. Like many who retire, he felt that he had been badly treated. Father Hesburgh's question was predicated on the assumption that, retired or not, Gabriel would continue to be a presence in the institute. Under his directorship, the library had become enriched. Most amazing of all, he had acquired on microfilm all the medieval manuscripts of the Biblioteca Ambrosiana in Milan, as well as thousands of photographs of Renaissance art. When Paul VI was Cardinal Montini of Milan he had been given an honorary degree by Notre Dame, and when he was shown the Medieval Institute, he said something about the Ambrosiana. The Ambrosiana, though it was in Milan, was not under the control of the cardinal. If he had suggested the microfilm project, he was not in a position to promise anything. No matter. Gabriel went into action.

The Ambrosiana was founded by the nephew of St. Charles Borromeo, who figures in Alessandro Manzoni's *I Promessi Sposi*. It is both a library and an art gallery—there is lock of Lucrezia Borgia's golden hair in its museum. Angelo Paredi was the director, and there was a small number of elected fellows. The place was theirs in which to work. Visitors could come, but they were guests in a very exclusive little club. When Gabriel arrived, the notion that the Ambrosiana manuscripts would be subjected to microfilming was dismissed. Manuscripts are fragile things, and who knew what such a filming would do to them? A lesser man would have desisted. Gabriel began to woo and cajole, he wined and dined, he became friends of Paredi, and the project of microfilming began. But it is no easy matter to take art works or their facsimiles out of Italy. Gabriel's diplomatic talents were then directed toward customs agents and the constabulary, and more wine flowed. This project, which was to take twenty years to complete, brought to Notre Dame not only a set of microfilms but, more importantly, a negative set from which further copies could be made. No one but Astrik Gabriel could have translated the perhaps polite remark of Cardinal Montini into the actuality of those two sets of microfilms containing all the medieval manuscripts of that magnificent Milanese library. If that were all Gabriel had done, it would have earned him the gratitude of his university.

Father Hesburgh had a deep sense of this debt, and while he could not waive the requirement that Gabriel retire, he did not intend to abandon him. I should also say that Gabriel was a priest of the Order of Premontré, the Premonstatensions as they are called by friends. Their foes have turned this into Monstrous Pretensions. The order has several foundations in the United States, but Gabriel's career had turned him into a wild card. There could not be any talk of returning to his community because the one in Hungary was in communist hands, and he had never been a member of any American community. So he would continue to have rooms on campus and an office on the seventh floor, and any new director would have to take into account this formidable figure.

My predecessor, Jeffrey Russell, who in any case was in the job only two years, did not adequately soothe Gabriel's spirit. I made it a priority to honor the man who was responsible for the wonderful institute I was to direct. And we got along. It might be said that I flattered him, buttered him up, soothed his ruffled feathers which were so easily soon ruffled again. Or it could be said, I hope more accurately, that I exhibited an appropriate *pietas* toward an accomplished scholar whose reputation was global. Or some of each. But we did get along. Gabriel settled more comfortably into his seventh-floor office, from time to time he would progress noisily through the reading room, but Lazenby had gone to God, and Gabriel was merely showing the flag. And he loved being seated in a place of honor when a visiting lecturer came. It was the rare lecturer who did not heap praise upon him.

Perhaps it was during my first year that I made a trip to Toronto, as a courtesy visit to the medieval center of which ours was a spinoff. Father Edward Synan, the director, was an old friend, and we had a pleasant get-together. He was taking me through the university library when I noticed a plaque on a door that read "Professor Dr. Astrik L. Gabriel." I stopped. "That's Gabe's office," Synan said. "He insisted on it in order to come back here." Come back? Gabriel, it emerged, was covering his bets, ensconcing himself in Toronto as well as at Notre Dame, unsure which way the winds would blow. Well, I thought, if my country had been invaded first by Nazis and then by Communists, my outlook too might resemble that of Janus. And it turned out that Gabriel himself was in Toronto. When I got back to my hotel room, there was a bottle of wine, fruit, and a note to call Gabriel. I did, and we had a memorable dinner—ordeal by wine—and he took me to his apartment to show me what his niece had done for him. It was lovely. We parted, and I went home and kept my peace, wondering if I would have to get along with Gabriel after all.

Gabriel's bargaining chip was always his personal collection of rare books. These were always discreetly referred to when he negotiated either in Toronto or Notre Dame. I learned that these volumes had been shipped to Toronto. So what portended? Then boxes began to arrive from Toronto, followed by the owner of the books they contained. Gabriel's seventh-floor office soon overflowed with these treasures. Gabriel was back.

■ I will mention a final editorial job, that of the quarterly of the Fellowship of Catholic Scholars. When I took it over it was a newsletter, but I had it redesigned, called it a quarterly, and had it handsomely printed. I have recently taken on this task again after a hiatus of a few years, but with the design work of Paul Wieber and the Renaissance talents of Alice Osberger, it is not an onerous task. What if I had never received that printing set when I was a boy, or the little tinny typewriter on which I produced a neighborhood paper? Perhaps the world would have been a better place, but I would have been a less happy man.

INTERNATIONAL
CATHOLIC UNIVERSITY

JUST BEFORE *EX CORDE ECCLESIAE* CAME OUT IN 1990, I WAS ASKED TO
take part in a symposium on Catholic higher education on a campus that
shall be nameless—alas, it could have been any of dozens. Just before
leaving home I had the good fortune of receiving an advance copy of the
document. How better address the topic of the symposium than by reference to this authoritative statement? When I rose to speak, I mentioned my good fortune in having the long awaited document with me
and based what I had to say on it. The reaction was instructive. Angry theologians rose to reject the papal document as irrelevant to our concerns.
One particularly agitated fellow began, in the manner of Charles Curran,
to tick off what he described as benighted positions of the Church over
the years, with particular reference to scriptural studies. His point seemed
to be that *Ex Corde Ecclesiae* had been issued by a fallible institution with
a long record of being on the wrong side of issues. Of course these unhappy theologians had at the time only my account of the document,
but it was not so much its contents as the fact that it had been issued that

they addressed. Indocility, even hostility, to the magisterium seemed to characterize the assembly.

I would have been surprised to be surprised. I recognized the reaction as merely another expression of the culture of dissent among theologians. When those whose role in the university is to teach and explain Catholic doctrine react in this way to a magisterial document, it is little wonder that other departments are influenced and come to think that "official" Catholic teaching has nothing to do with their teaching. Critics of *Ex Corde Ecclesiae* invoked the tradition of academic freedom, seen as incompatible with the Church presuming to offer guidelines to those in the business of Catholic higher education. Of course, the pope himself had related what he was saying to academic freedom, "rightly understood," and failed to see the conflict decried by the dissenters. Their conception of academic freedom entailed that no one outside the university community could authoritatively address that community or presume to tell it how to behave. The net result of this, of course, is the denial that there is any essential difference between secular and Catholic higher education. St. Mary's of the Babbling Brook had no more reason to attend to *Ex Corde Ecclesiae* than did Meatball Tech. How better summarize what has been called the secularization of Catholic higher education?

Books have been written on this subject, following in the wake of other books that had discussed the secularization of the universities founded by various Protestant denominations. There is no need for me to summarize those studies. The phenomenon is captured in the contention that religious faith can play no role in higher education because, in seeking to guide it from the "outside," it violates academic freedom. The prospect before us when this view dominates is the eradication of any difference between Catholic and secular higher education. Nor will I repeat the obvious response to this that universities and colleges are in their very nature guided by accrediting boards, professional societies, and a host of other interested parties "outside" the university. Imagine a medical school that bristled at the idea that the American Medical Association might make demands on its curriculum. The apparent upshot of these observations is to notice that there is only one outside authority that is rejected, and that is the magisterium of the Catholic Church.

Permit me to be repetitive. I have spent my academic career in what I regard as the premier institution of Catholic higher education in this country, Notre Dame. I have seen close up, and have participated in, decisions that have had the unlooked-for effect of sending us down the path of secularization. Years ago, John Tracy Ellis, an eminent Church historian, wrote a piece that became a booklet and stirred up much discussion on Catholic campuses. Ellis invoked a number of criteria of excellence in higher education, such as winning Nobel prizes, and found Catholic institutions woefully behind their secular counterparts. He was taken to mean that we must bend our best efforts to bettering ourselves, to becoming excellent.

Quite apart from the criteria chosen, it would be difficult to oppose the suggestion that excellence in what we are doing should be our watchword. But the effect of Ellis's piece was to locate excellence in secular higher education, and from this there followed the tendency to take those institutions as models for the upgrading of our colleges and universities. Eventually, it became commonplace at Notre Dame to speak of, say, Stanford, as our peer institution, with the implication that there are common criteria of excellent performance on both campuses. And what was wrong with that?

It was based on two assumptions, the first at the time only implicit— if it had been explicitly stated, it would have been repudiated—and this was that it is the faith that is holding us back from excellence. By the time of *Ex Corde Ecclesiae*, the implicit had become explicit: the faith, or at least the magisterium, was an impediment to doing our job well. Hence the reaction at the symposium mentioned above.

The second assumption was that everything was going well on those secular campuses which were looked to as the repositories of excellence. But it was not long before book after book appeared questioning this assumption. In the meantime, Catholic institutions endeavored to hire the products of those "excellent" institutions, with the idea that we could, if not lick them, then join them by filling our faculties with those who had received their graduate education from them. Even apart from the critique of such institutions in books like Alan Bloom's *The Closing of the American Mind,* and thinking only of my own field, philosophy, this hiring policy involved difficulties. One of the basic motives for Leo XIII's *Aeterni Patris* had been the judgment that modern society was getting deeper and deeper into trouble because it was grounded in modern philosophy. But no such misgivings could be found in the graduate schools devoted precisely to teaching and developing the principles that Leo had seen as incompatible with the faith.

Take an example. Modern and contemporary moral philosophy accepted as good money the tenet that the way things are, the way we are, is irrelevant to judgments of moral good and evil. Divorced from fact and unmoored in nature, moral philosophy underwrote moral relativism. If you and I disagree in our judgments on some moral matter, no appeal to what we are talking about can adjudicate our differences. To take a divisive issue, you think abortion is permitted and I think it forbidden. No appeal to what an abortion is and what performing it effects can establish the truth of my claim and the falsity of yours. But of course the reverse must also be true. What then is the source of our moral judgments? Intuitionism was tried: you just see the good in the way you see yellow. But this did not address the fact that, in the moral order, we have a habit of seeing different things. Utilitarianism was tried: to say that something is good or bad is to say something about the consequences of doing it. If by and large an act or kind of act is beneficial to the majority, that is all the justification one needs to call it good. The insuperable problem here lies in predicting consequences. Judgments of moral good and bad become prophecies, and only the future will tell whether what I am doing now is a good thing to do. When the difficulties with intuitionism and utilitarianism were acknowledged, emotivism won the day. That is, judgments of good and bad are to be taken as expressions of the speaker's feelings or subjective condition. This being the case, moral judgments could only be taken to have public value at the price of tyranny. That is, to promote a moral position is to seek to make others act in accord with your feelings about the matter. Here is the root of the privatization of morality along with religion. In the public square there must be neutrality with respect to substantive moral judgments. Adjudications took the form of according each moral position an equal value and making sure that none gained precedence over the others.

Any effort to build a society on such a view is an invitation to chaos or at least incoherence. Or, the more sinister possibility, since no view is true and one holds the view one does, one will seek to win the day by force.

If we were engaged in philosophizing as such, everything I have said would need to be expanded, refined, take into account possible objections, and so on. But in the end we would find that the finer-grained analysis had brought us to the conclusion I reached with unbecoming philosophical swiftness. The triumph of emotivism can be discerned in newspaper editorials, op-ed pages, political debates, *partout*. Bloom and

Alasdair MacIntyre, in different ways, make this point, and they have since been joined by a chorus of others. But isn't the rejection of relativism itself an expression of a subjective conviction and thus unable to exclude its opposite? The most interesting discussions in recent moral philosophy have had to do with this response to the critique of moral relativism. And so we have been driven back to the technique that Plato used against Protagoras. The great sophist had maintained that what is true for you is true for you and what is true for me is true for me. Plato argued that this claim is incoherent. It refutes itself. Its refutation comes not from an alien viewpoint, but from its own internal assumptions.

One could go on. I have said as much as I have only to illustrate the untenability of the dominant view in modern moral philosophy. While it is true that some who were introduced to philosophy in this context fought their way free of it and found it untenable, the majority try to make do with what they have been taught, doubtless thinking that there is no alternative to it. For a Catholic, from the very outset, moral relativism is recognized as untenable. The acceptance of it would make mincemeat of the assumptions of his faith. Of course this recognition does not provide him with any detailed argument against moral relativism, and some believers must busy themselves with the refutation of it lest those believers without the skill or time be misled.

Those final sentences in the preceding paragraph will fuel the worst fears of nonbelievers and of those who hold that faith is irrelevant to reason. Don't they reveal that the believer has a closed mind, that he is not open to positions in conflict, real or apparent, with his religious beliefs? The believer is seen as one who comes to philosophy burdened with a mass of presuppositions which prevent him from following the argument wherever it might go. The initial assumption of philosophizing from Descartes on—with of course notable exceptions—has been that before beginning one must first sweep one's mind clear of all presuppositions. On this view, the real philosopher is one who, at the outset at least, must operate as if he has no given starting points. The search for a starting point is the beginning of philosophy. *De omnibus dubitandum est.* The problem with this project is that its realization is impossible. A mind scrubbed clear of all convictions is a chimera. The nonbeliever, like the believer, begins philosophy on the basis of assumptions taken to be true. The aim of methodic doubt was to arrive at a claim that could not be doubted—in the case of Descartes, that he was thinking, no matter if whatever he thought was false. But what is thinking? What is truth, what is falsity? Along the route of methodic doubt there are unacknowledged and undoubted assumptions that some things are true and others false. If there are no instances of true and false judgment, the terms lose their meaning.

Moving right along, we arrive at the disturbing realization that no one is free of antecedent assumptions. The believer has his, the nonbeliever has his. Philosophizing then seems to be an effort to justify those assumptions, with the result that theories reflect antecedent assumptions. But antecedent assumptions vary and conflict. Philosophy thus seems relativized. Philosophical disagreement is merely a function of conflicting antecedent assumptions. But then we come back to Plato and Protagoras.

The believer's response to the charge against him thus seems to be hurling a *tu quoque* at the nonbeliever. Philosophizing of a sort can take place without resolving this standoff. One concentrates on the logic involved in moving off from assumptions, whatever they might be. But that turns out to be the way out the woods. Logic at least must seem common to those who disagree. Looking into the presuppositions of logic—that there is an opposition between the true and false, for example—leads to the recognition of pre-logical truths. Thus, there is light at the end of the tunnel and there seems to be a way out of the impasse of relativism. The fact that those who disagree must share a common language in order to do so is another indication of the possibility of adjudicating philosophical disputes by appeal to the objective.

Such considerations as these bring us to the value of faith as a presupposition of philosophizing. The believer has a powerful motivation to undertake the task sketched in the preceding paragraphs. He begins with the certainty that claims in conflict with the truth of faith must be false, and his task is to pay off on that certainty in a way that is in principle acceptable to those with whom initially he is in disagreement. The Church cannot responsibly be indifferent to the claims of philosophers in conflict with the deposit of faith. That is why believers are counseled to begin philosophizing in a way that will equip them for that polemical task. But the refutation of error is a byproduct, not the ultimate point of philosophizing.

I have portrayed the conflict as one between believer and nonbeliever, but the hiring policy mentioned earlier has brought the battle within the walls of Catholic higher education. In Catholic departments of philosophy, one now has tenured colleagues whose training disposes them to take seriously positions which, however implicitly, are in conflict with the faith. And of course, students in our colleges and universities are likely to be taught by professors whose views, if true, would undermine the student's faith. That is why those of us who have spent long careers in traditional Catholic institutions are involved in a long twilight struggle within the walls. Positions dubiously compatible with the faith are maintained and taught all around us. A young colleague of mine announced in a departmental meeting that, since he regarded Catholicism as false, he had a moral obligation to disabuse his students of their faith. That is where we have come.

■   Over the years, when I have mentioned to students the documents of Vatican II and the many magisterial documents since, I have been met with blank stares. They would say that they have never heard of them, not even in theology courses. There was no need to take these remarks as accurate portrayals of what the theology department was offering in order to respond to the curiosity of such students. Accordingly, I arranged evening seminars in the Maritain Center devoted to reading and discussion of the sixteen conciliar documents and some of the great encyclicals of John Paul II. As many as twenty students would take part. These seminars became the most heartening experience of my twilight years at Notre Dame. Eventually, these meetings were formalized as directed reading courses and were accepted as such by the theology department, as well as by my own. Of late, there has been less need of these, given a great sea change taking place among our younger theologians, and yet they go on. I find that I would be very reluctant to deprive myself of those evenings with these students, among the best and brightest in the university, who are eager to furnish their minds with elements of Catholic culture. By and large, students come to Notre Dame because it is a Catholic university, and many are disappointed by the apparent absence of anything specifically Catholic in our course offerings. They resolve to do something about it. For some years now, there has been a renaissance of sorts among undergraduates, young people who cannot accept the notion that an education at Notre Dame should be indistinguishable from that in secular universities. This manifests itself in the formation of prayer groups and retreats as well as in the pursuit of knowledge. And this of course is the way things should be in a Catholic university. Education is more than what would now be called a head trip; it is the formation of a person, it is one form of the pursuit of holiness.

Many of the students involved in the Maritain Center seminars are products of Catholic education, both grade school and high school, before coming to Notre Dame. They are gifted, they are intellectually curious, but often they are all but illiterate in things Catholic. One of the ironies of these years when Vatican II has been invoked on the left and on the right is that few seem to have any idea what went on at the Council and what it actually taught. The only defense against the false spirit of Vatican II is to acquire the true spirit.

To address the illiteracy among Catholics in the wider world, the Maritain Center began the so-called Basics of Catholicism, week-long summer seminars at which stellar figures in promoting the true spirit of Vatican II gave crash courses in the elements of Catholic culture. The participants, never more than a hundred at a time, were housed in a student residence on campus. We gathered for Mass each morning and also said together the morning and evening prayers of the Church. The days were full. Monsignor William Smith laid out the main lines of the magisterium of John Paul II as well as of moral theology. Father Kenneth Baker led a barefoot trip through the Bible. Father Fessio spoke on the liturgy, Marvin O'Connell and Jim Hitchcock on various historical issues. Helen Hitchcock, Janet Smith, and Laura Garcia spoke on family and women's issues. Gerry Bradley and Charles Rice discussed legal and constitutional questions. Jim Holman, an early participant, returned as a speaker and told of his publishing efforts in California. As is usually the case in such summer conferences, the informal meetings with like-minded people from around the country and the chance to shoot the bull with the speakers over an evening beer were at least as important as the formal sessions.

Bishop John D'Arcy spoke at the first conference, and in later years his auxiliary, Bishop Crowley, said a Mass for the participants. The sanction of the local bishop was essential to an effort aimed at conveying Church doctrine, something that should never be seen as a freelance enterprise, independent of the authority of the successors of the Apostles. The conferences went on for over a decade. Connie's illness became terminal in the spring of 2002, so the conference scheduled for that summer had to be canceled. As it turned out, 2001 was the final conference.

Once the continuity had been broken, to resume presented problems. The speakers who had been so generous with their time for so long were of course extremely busy people. They had left room in their schedule for the Basics of Catholicism, but the hiatus for some provided an occasion for yet other involvements. I felt that the Basics had perhaps accomplished all it could. A problem was that when people came for one conference, they wanted to come back the next year. But the point had been to provide a beginning, a spur, not an annual summer get-together. I understood this desire. I myself listened to every talk at every conference. One of the bonuses of the conferences was that the participants lived on campus and got a feel for Notre Dame. Some came with the notion that Notre Dame could be summed up in the views of a few voluble dissenters whose television appearances mistakenly made them seem the spokesmen for the university. But to walk the campus walks, to visit the Basilica of the Sacred Heart and the grotto, to walk around St. Joseph and St. Mary lakes, to feed the ducks, perhaps to stroll out to the community cemetery where one could not help but be aware of the heroes and heroines who had hallowed this place, had their effect. People left with a very different sense of Notre Dame than they had anticipated.

And so I conceived the notion of the International Catholic University, and if the initials suggest the intensive care unit, so be it. It occurred to me that in our universities are many who have their heads on straight— diaspora Catholics, if you will—however they may seem to be outnumbered in their institutions. Gathering them all into one place was literally impossible, so it was necessary to do it virtually. By this time, so-called distance education was underway. Why not have a Catholic university accessible electronically, bringing the Catholic patrimony to anyone with a computer, a VCR, or an audio cassette player? I put the matter to Mother Angelica, the founder of EWTN (Eternal Word Television Network), on a visit to Birmingham, and she invited me onto her program to announce the formation of this university. EWTN would participate by making its studios available to our professors, where their lectures would be filmed and edited. In the course of the program, a caller wanted to know if we would teach Latin. Of course, I said. That sanguine response was the genesis of a little book, *Let's Read Latin, Introduction to the Language of the Church*, a Dumb Ox imprint. I took the caller to be wondering how broad a spectrum ICU would represent in its offerings.

My original idea had not envisaged courses taken for credit. In asking around, I had been told that 60 percent of the people who sign up for such courses simply want to learn; credits and degrees are not the point. Mother Angelica disagreed. She believed, rightly I came to think, that without the possibility of gaining credit, the courses would not have sufficient éclat even for those who simply wanted to learn. And so began the long process of becoming accredited. Thanks to the State of Connecticut and our connection with Holy Apostles Seminary in Cromwell, not only can credits be earned, but we have M.A. programs in both philosophy and theology. Many of the courses available in video and audio do not figure in these sequences, and for now they are taken by people who simply want to learn. ICU has gotten this far. I would like to see it become a full-scale virtual university, with an undergraduate and doctoral program. The undergraduate degree would be in the great books, the liberal arts; it would not be feasible to have the many departments of a college. As for the doctoral program, it isn't hard to guess.

All this may seem impossible, but then so did ICU at the outset. If there is one thing I have learned from Mother Angelica and Father Fessio, two of the brightest stars in the Church today, it is that good ideas ought to be pursued, and then one of two things happens. Either they work out or they don't. If they don't, try another. Man proposes, God disposes.

ON THE BANKS OF
THE MAINSTREAM

NOT LONG AGO I WENT TO THE VIGIL MASS AT ST. PIUS X, A LOCAL parish I sometimes avail myself of rather than drive to campus. Father Dan Scheidt, the associate pastor, who was vested and waiting to go down the main aisle to say the Mass, turned and saw me come in. An almost startled expression crossed his face, and then he came over and asked tentatively, "Are you by any chance related to Ralph McInerny?" "Yes," I said. "By identity." The answer convinced him. He had been a student of mine at Notre Dame, and sufficient time had passed to lead him to think that it had been a memorable experience.

I have not always been identical with Ralph McInerny. Back in my days of writing magazine fiction, stories first printed in American magazines were often sold for reprinting in European magazines. Once, after a story of mine had appeared in England, I received an indignant letter, forwarded to me by an editor of the magazine in which it had been reprinted. It was from a retired army officer living in Portugal who objected to my attaching his name to so ephemeral a piece. Signed, Ralph McInerny. I wrote him a witty letter, to which he did not reply. Obviously an imposter.

Writing a letter to Ralph McInerny—surely an unusual combination of names—was an odd experience. Almost as odd as having written all these pages about myself. As I bring the account to a close I find that I have been an elusive subject, or several subjects going by the same name.

Jean Oesterle spent her last year in a nursing home, and it was easy for me to visit her since the place was located between our house and Notre Dame. After she had been there half a year, declining all the while, something in her manner made me ask, "Jean, do you know who I am?" She looked at me for a while and then leaned toward me, looking anxious. "Don't you know?" I laughed, she laughed, but maybe she had a point.

The point of a proper name is that it not common to many, and yet many people do bear identical names. Aristotle said the purpose of language was to tame the uncountability of things by bringing them under a manageable number of words. But even when two persons have the same proper name it does not become a common noun, like "man." All the John Smiths that have been, are, and will be have nothing in common but the name; it does not name something common to them all. There is an inescapable nominalism here. God calls us all by our proper name, and He is unlikely to confuse one John Smith with another. A mother duck quacks, and only some of the seemingly identical ducklings come to her. She knows them and they know her. It goes deeper with people, who are persons. Each is unique.

That we have a common nature, the same in all, is far from a complete account of us. There are those who have been tempted by this realization to embrace the theory that we each have an individual essence, more profound than that we share with others of our species. A pardonable mistake, I suppose, but it carries with it Leibnitzean consequences, among them determinism. If everything about me is essential to me, it must follow that I really was not free to do those things I did and did not do. In fact, the imagined individual essence, unlike that of the species, is a congeries of incidental truths. We are what we do and thus might have, by acting otherwise, made a self quite different from the one we have fashioned.

For all that, we are what we have done, and not even God can undo the past, so if one hankers for necessity, it is here. But looking back on that unchangeable past, one is struck by how easily it might have been otherwise. And if that is not vertiginous enough, think of the happenstance of your parents meeting and marrying and bearing wonderful you. And their parents and theirs, and theirs, back into the immemorial past. Whenever I visit Ennis in County Clare I am haunted by the thought of ancestors whose names I will never know, without whose cooings and couplings I would never have been. There was no Ralph among them, so far as I know. Aldous Huxley has a poem in which he writes of the act of coition wherein out of a "million million" spermatazoa, "but one poor Noah / Dare hope to survive," and that "One was Me." The past has a randomness that can overwhelm, yet through it all the invisible hand of God has operated.

■   My parents were Oblates of St. Benedict and my mother, at least, said each day the little office. She also went to daily Mass, at which our pastor, Father Rowan, would commemorate in a loud voice "Archbishop Ireland, who ordained me." In her missal she kept a number of mementos, among them love notes from my father written before their marriage on September 1, 1926. My brother Dennis, who now has the missal, sent me copies of some of them. They are typed. "Dear Vivian, I LOVE YOU. Your husband, Austin. 17 more days. Wowie." And there is a full-page letter, typed on the stationery of M. P. McInerny, Heating and Plumbing, July 26, '26.

> Dear Madame,
>   Your remittance in settlement of my account against you amounting to One Hundred and Seventy-Five Millions Kisses has not been received. I have been endeavoring to evidence a very liberal policy in this matter. However, I feel that the time has come when I must insist upon settlement in full at our next meeting.

The conceit is pursued for paragraphs and ends with the instruction that she appear at Holy Name Church on September 1, 1926, where they will marry and thus afford her a convenient way to pay her debt.

It is an odd experience for an old man to read the lovesick missives of his twenty-three-year-old father. He outlived my mother by nine years, living on in the house they had bought for four thousand dollars when I was in the eighth grade and where they had raised their family. My brother Denny joined the philosophy department at the University of St. Thomas in St. Paul and lived with him during those last years, so the rest of us were relieved of concern about his day-to-day existence. He devoted himself to watercolors after an unsuccessful oil portrait of my mother over which he labored with too much love. All of us have in our homes pictures he painted then. I have, as well, a framed thank-you card containing a self-portrait in pencil under which he had printed, Benefit of the Doubt. Having known the loneliness that comes with outliving Connie, I now recall my visits to my aged father with remorse. I don't think I had any inkling of how devastating it was for him to lose my mother. Whenever I visited him we always seemed to end up arguing about some nonsensical thing. Now I think of him painting into the wee hours, alone, a grumpy romantic of that heroic generation that survived the Great Depression.

Recently I visited my daughter Mary and was looking at the pictures in her living room and came upon a self-portrait I had done in pencil, framed. I had no memory of doing it. After Connie died, I found in the table beside her bed a letter I had written in the summer of 1954 from Quebec where I was teaching English. How I missed her. I told her that we would have another honeymoon in Omaha. I feel more and more like my father.

■   Why the title of this concluding section? The things that have occupied me over the years have seldom been influenced by the zeitgeist, except negatively. As a Thomist, I have pursued a line quite different from the dominant one in Anglo-American philosophy, let alone Continental philosophy. And I have lived to see my way of doing philosophy become an oddity in the department to which I have belonged for half a century. My graduate work at Minnesota provided the occasion for a conscious choice to return to Thomas. The rationale of Leo XIII's *Aeterni Patris* has proved its soundness to me over the years. There is no other way, really. *Gustate et videte.* Water only slakes when drunk, and the choice we make at the outset of philosophizing is a fateful one. Of course I was guided by the Church in the direction I took and not only by the sense that what I had learned at Minnesota did not promise a satisfying alternative. But I knew I was turning away from the sort of thing that dominated Anglo-American philosophy.

Long ago at Nazareth Hall, Father James Shannon had us use *Return to Tradition* by Francis Beauchesne Thornton as a textbook in an English course. The anthology was heavy with selections from the Catholic literary revival in Europe and in English-speaking countries, and its message, as I read it, was: we are the mainstream. Only writers whose work is in continuity with the great tradition stretching back to the ages of faith, to Shakespeare and Dante and Chaucer, are in the true mainstream of our civilization. I learned to look differently at the great modern writers, seeing them in the shallower waters along the shore. It was no accident that Longfellow translated the *Divine Comedy*. Graham Greene, after his conversion, devoted several essays to Henry James, on the *qui vive* for the Master's attitude toward the faith he would have found all around him in the Europe of his choice. Edwin Fussel's *Henry James and Catholicism* is an exhaustive pursuit of this same idea. Yankees who could not warm to the immigrant Catholicism around them often suspected during their European sojourns that it was Protestantism that is marginal. The heroine of Charlotte Bronte's novel *Villette*, set in Brussels, goes into a church and into the confessional to whisper her sins. This is balanced, I suppose, by the mad wife of Mr. Rochester, who seems to have been a Catholic. Such converts as Greene and Fussel notice these things. And so do cradle Catholics.

The formative Catholicism of F. Scott Fitzgerald fascinated me, as did Hemingway's flirtation with the faith after his second marriage. *The Sun Also Rises* contrasts the mindless hedonism of its main characters with the implications of the feast of San Firmin. And of course T. S. Eliot, if not Ezra Pound, was ours. Robert Lowell's *Lord Weary's Castle* was shaped by his Catholicism (when my copy arrived at Nazareth Hall, Father Karl Wittman noticed it and revealed himself to be a kindred spirit), and there were the Fugitives and eventually Flannery O'Connor and Walker Percy. And of course, J. F. Powers. Thomas Merton's *Seven Storey Mountain* was a goodbye to all that of a different sort from Robert Graves's, a turning away from the alleged mainstream to the real one. James Joyce, the peering apostate, represented the tragic consequences of trying to make a religion of art, trying to form in the smithy of his soul the uncreated conscience of his race.

Catholicism in recent American fiction seems to function largely as an abandoned faith, a thing of childhood now set aside. I see in this another consequence of the post-conciliar drift toward secularization, an abandonment of the true wellspring of creativity. The dominant culture becomes ever more hostile, not only to the supernatural but to the common morality that true religion presupposes and reinforces. And born Catholic writers abandon the faith of their fathers to accommodate themselves to its contradictory. I find this tragic. Fiction is an imaginative presentation of what it is to be a human person. When it loses its sense of our ultimate destiny, when it is devoid of the fundamental moral outlook which alone gives weight to the deeds of men, it loses more than its soul.

In these last years I think of the irony of my own case. As a philosopher, I have been blessed by a recognition, however modest, that I would never have had if I had taken a different path. The invitation to translate and edit a selection of the writings of Thomas Aquinas for Penguin Classics would obviously not have come. Nor would the invitation to deliver the Gifford lectures in Glasgow in 1999–2000. On another level was my appointment to the President's Committee on Art and the Humanities. The Liberty Fund included me in its Intellectual Portrait Series of filmed interviews, with Jody Bottum serving as my interlocutor. But the one honor I cherish above all others was my election as a fellow of the Pontifical Academy of St. Thomas Aquinas. By contrast, I have seen many of my contemporaries who set their sails to prevailing winds become lost in the huge regatta taking its bearings from the Titanic. My own is a minor case, but I think of those giants of my youth, Thomists all, whose names were on the lips of everyone. In one of his huge collections, *More Matter*, John Updike mentions several times his awareness as a Harvard undergraduate of the way Jacques Maritain had made Scholasticism something one had to take seriously. Not that I think the intrinsic value of what we do is to be measured by such contingent recognition, but after all, one writes to be read, and the decent respect of mankind is not an ignoble aspiration.

There is an inevitable valedictory tone to these valedictory remarks, but I cannot say that I think my work is done. In 1996, after giving a talk in Woodstock, Illinois, I stopped to see my daughter Cathy and her family in Barrington. After I left, she called her mother to say how sick I seemed. It was more than seeming. Connie hustled me off to the doctor, and soon I was being wheeled into the operating room for a triple bypass. It sounded like something on the Interstate. Some months later I sat next to a doctor at a dinner in Washington. He had heard of my operation and cheerily predicted that I might have several more years of life. I was astounded, feeling that my usual good health had been fully restored. It was not until January of 2003 that I had a heart attack. I drove myself to the hospital and told them in emergency I thought I was having a heart attack. I was. Things were rectified with angioplasty. Despite all this, I still have trouble thinking of myself as mortal. "Thou fool, this very night thy soul shall be required of thee." Still, one soldiers on, heading into a future, which however truncated in my case, and always of course obscure, beckons. *So we beat on, boats against the current, borne back ceaselessly into the past.*